WARRIOR • 167

EARLY AEGEAN WARRIOR 5000–1450 BC

RAFFAELE D'AMATO AND ANDREA SALIMBETI   ILLUSTRATED BY GIUSEPPE RAVA

Series editor Marcus Cowper

First published in Great Britain in 2013 by Osprey Publishing,
Midland House, West Way, Botley, Oxford OX2 0PH, UK
43-01 21st Street, Suite 220B, Long Island City, NY 11101, USA
E-mail: info@ospreypublishing.com

A CIP catalogue record for this book is available from the British Library.

ISBN: 978 1 78096 858 2
E-book ISBN: 978 1 78096 860 5
PDF ISBN: 978 1 78096 859 9

Editorial by Ilios Publishing Ltd, Oxford, UK (www.iliospublishing.com)
Index by Zoe Ross
Typeset in Myriad Pro and Sabon
Artwork by Giuseppe Rava
Originated by PDQ Media, UK
Printed in China through Worldprint Ltd

13 14 15 16 17 10 9 8 7 6 5 4 3 2 1

www.ospreypublishing.com

DEDICATION

To Paola Cassola Guida, a great teacher and scholar of Aegean weaponry.

ACKNOWLEDGEMENTS

The authors would like to thank all the scholars and friends who have
helped in the realization of this book, as well as the museums and
institutes visited.

A particular acknowledgement is due to Lucia Alberti (PHD) of the Istituto
di Studi sulle civiltà dell'Egeo e del Vicino Oriente (ICEVO) at the Consiglio
Nazionale delle ricerche of Rome for her help in supplying important
iconographic material.

The authors would especially like to thank the following institutes and
museums: the National Archaeological Museum of Athens, the Volos
Archaeological Museum, the Iraklion Museum, the British Museum, the
Louvre Museum, the Archaeological Museum of Khanià, the ICEVO Library
and the Library of the Deutsches Archäologisches Institut of Athens.

The authors are deeply grateful also to Stefanie Groener (BA) for linguistic
assistance and help in editing the English text.

Finally, special acknowledgement must be given to the illustrator
Giuseppe Rava, who has brought to the life the Aegean ancient world
in such a lavish manner.

ARTIST'S NOTE

Readers may care to note that the original paintings from which the
colour plates in this book were prepared are available for private sale.
The Publishers retain all reproduction copyright whatsoever. All enquiries
should be addressed to:

Giuseppe Rava, Via Borgotto 17, 18018 Faenza (RA), Italy
www.g-rava.it
info@g-rava.it

The Publishers regret that they can enter into no correspondence upon
this matter.

ABBREVIATIONS

BSA = British School of Athens
EC = Early Cycladic
EM = Early Minoan
MM = Medium Minoan
JbRGZM = Jahrbuch des Römisch-Germanischen Zentralmuseum Mainz
LM = Late Minoan
LH = Late Helladic
P.A.C.T. Journal = Professional Association of Classroom Teachers Magazine

THE WOODLAND TRUST

Osprey Publishing are supporting the Woodland Trust, the UK's leading
woodland conservation charity, by funding the dedication of trees.

CONTENTS

EARLY AEGEAN WARRIOR 5000–1450 BC

INTRODUCTION

Evidence of human settlements in the Aegean region dates as far back as prehistoric times. Their origin and development was modelled in terms of large-scale processes (such as agriculture and urbanization) and by the progress of civilization.

Mainland culture

The Greek mainland Neolithic settlement of Sesklo on Kastraki Hill dates from the middle of the 7th to the 4th millennium BC. Sesklo, discovered at the end of the 19th century, is considered one of the main Neolithic settlements in Europe. The pottery found there forms the chronological basis for the Middle Neolithic sub-periods for the whole Hellenic region ('Sesklo civilization'). Its main features are the improved firing technique used for clay pottery, which produces a superb red colour, and the use of stone tools, weapons and obsidian, imported from Melos. The people of this period lived by raising animals and farming. In the Early Neolithic Period (6th millennium BC), the houses had stone foundations, walls of unbaked mud-brick and floors of beaten clay.

The hill of Dimini – one of the better-known Greek Neolithic settlements – was inhabited almost from the beginning of the 5th millennium BC and gradually evolved until 4500 BC. It has been reckoned that there were 200 or at most 300 inhabitants. Among its archaeological remains (architecture, pottery, tools, figurines, jewellery), all cultural achievements of the Aegean society of the Late Neolithic II Period (4800–4500 BC) are represented (Dimini Culture of Greek Prehistory).

Cyclades

According to the findings, the Cyclades had been inhabited by a native population that had been arriving from the Greek mainland since the Mesolithic Era (7500–6500 BC). More accurate archaeology has revealed that a massive migration of a proto-Ionic farming and seafaring society, coming from Asia Minor, moved to the Cyclades around 5000 BC.

For the first time, these populations imported to the region the copper utilized to make weapons, tools and objects for everyday use. About 3000 BC a new wave of migration apparently occurred in the Aegean, most likely from Asia Minor. These people used bronze, a revolutionary material in ancient human history made from an alloy of copper and tin, thus introducing the Bronze Age. Early Cycladic civilization – the forerunner of the first true Greek culture – rises at about the same time as the early Egyptian and Mesopotamian civilizations.

Modern scholars conventionally divide it into three periods: Protocycladic (3200–2000 BC), Mesocycladic (2000–1550 BC) and Postcycladic (1150–1100 BC). During these phases Cycladic culture was at first increasingly swamped by the rising influence of Minoan Crete and later of Helladic Achaea.

Reconstructive drawing of the Dimini fortifications, about 5000 BC, Athens, National Archaeological Museum. (Author's collection)

Early Cyprus

The earliest traces of human activity on Cyprus, probably short-lived populations of hunter-gatherers, date to about 8800 BC. Though the evidence is sketchy it seems that these visiting bands exterminated the island's unique fauna and did not establish any permanent settlements.

The first permanent Neolithic settlements appeared towards the end of the 8th millennium BC and were inhabited by small communities of farmers, fishermen and hunters probably arriving from the Syro-Palestinian coast and Anatolia. This culture, which takes its name from the best-known site of the period, Khirokitia in the south, was short lived and had gone into decline by 5500 BC.

The second group of inhabitants, known as the Sotira culture, had no connection with its predecessors, even if it sometimes occupied the same sites. It is distinguished by small ornaments of picrolite (a variety of soapstone) and progressively more elaborate pottery, and lived in Cyprus between 4600 and 3900 BC. Its economy was based on agricultural trade between its villages but not with the outside world. Towards the end of this period copper came into use. The decline of this culture was rapid, perhaps precipitated at least in some places by an earthquake, and several sites were abandoned.

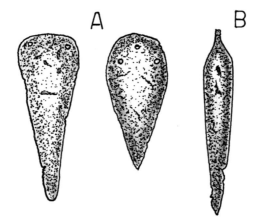

Selection of copper daggers from: a) Haghia Marina (Phocis), b) Haghios Dimitrios (Triphylia), Late-Final Neolithic (c.5300–3200 BC). Chaironeia Museum n. inv. 698α, 698β, Olympia Museum, M1324. (Drawing by Andrea Salimbeti ex Papathanasopoulos)

The succeeding era (3900–2500 BC) is known as the Chalcolithic Period (literally, copper-stone age). This period represents a transitional stage between the Neolithic and the Early Bronze Age, and is characterized by the appearance in Cyprus of the first metal objects, mainly small tools of hammered copper. It is still unclear whether copper-working was a local invention or imported from the East. There are no indications of systematic extraction of copper on Cyprus during this period. On the other hand, the evidence of maritime trade is limited to small quantities of obsidian from Asia Minor. The economy continued to be based on agriculture, although gradually developments such as the use of seals, the construction of special installations for worship and increasing diversity in burial habits appeared, suggesting relatively complex forms of social organization. Of particular interest are the abstract female figurines, fashioned from the local stone picrolite, which allude to fertility cults, continuing a long Neolithic tradition.

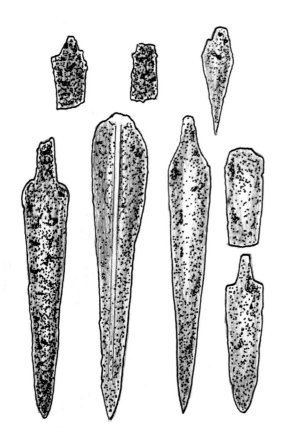

Selection of copper daggers from Dimini and Sesklo (c.4800–3300 BC). (Drawing by Andrea Salimbeti)

The transition from the Chalcolithic to the Early Bronze Age was marked by radical changes, most likely caused either by population migration from the coast of Asia Minor or by internal developments. Old settlements were abandoned and new ones were founded close to sources of water and tracts of arable land. The systematic exploitation of the rich copper ore deposits on the island began in this period with techniques of mining, smelting and working that were possibly introduced from the Near East, where metallurgy was already advanced. By the end of the Early Bronze Age, the Cypriot bronzesmiths had developed their own tradition, producing distinctive types of weapons and tools. Nonetheless, trade continued to be limited and farming continued to form the basis of the economy.

During the Middle Bronze Age, Cyprus developed more complex forms of social organization partly due to increased trading connections with neighbouring cultures. The pronounced differences in wealth, observed in burials, point to more strictly defined social divisions. Many settlements were fortified, probably in response to domestic conflicts

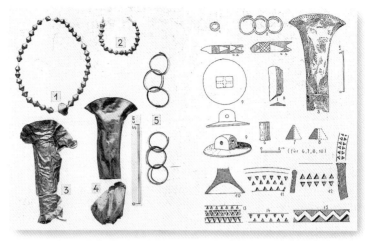

rather than to external threats. Religion acquired more complex forms of expression, with specific cult sites and elaborate ritual trappings. The presence of permanent metallurgical installations confirms the increasing importance of copper for the island and there is sound evidence of trade with the Syro-Palestinian coast, Egypt, Anatolia and Minoan Crete. Moreover, the earliest Mesopotamian and Egyptian texts referring to a 'copper-producing land called Alashiya' (identified as Cyprus by many scholars) date to this period.

During the Late Bronze Age, Cyprus came into its own as a major centre of copper production, supplying the entire Eastern Mediterranean. Urban settlements grew up close to the harbours from which copper ingots and bronze artefacts were shipped to the Aegean, the Middle East and Egypt to be bartered or exchanged for other products and luxury goods. In the larger cities, buildings were erected for administrative purposes, while a still-undeciphered system of writing (about 1500 BC) was adopted from Crete (Cypro-Minoan script), enabling the Cypriots to cope with the increasing bureaucratic need for inventories and archives.

Selection of weapons in copper and gold from Leukas, family grave R (4th millennium BC) ex Dorpfeld, 1927. (Author's collection)

Selection of bronze weapons, razors and arrow heads in obsidian from Leukas, family grave S (4th millennium BC) ex Dorpfeld, 1927. (Author's collection)

Crete

Minoan pre-Hellenic Bronze Age civilization originated with a mix of native people from the Greek mainland and from the Eastern Mediterranean, who are believed by some scholars to have migrated from Asia Minor to Crete and other islands of the Aegean Sea during the late Neolithic Period.

Different skull types discovered during excavation confirm the mix of racial elements in the Aegean islands (Asians, Africans and Europeans). In general terms, however, the Minoans form part of the so-called 'Mediterranean type';

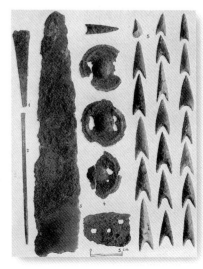

they were mainly of medium height and had black curly hair and brown eyes. The term 'Minoan' was used for the first time by the British archaeologist Sir Arthur Evans after the mythical King Minos, associated with the Labyrinth, which Evans identified as the Palace of Knossos. It is unknown what the Minoans called themselves, although the Egyptian place name *Keftiu* and the Semite *Kaftor* or *Caphtor* both evidently refer to Minoan Crete. In a later age the tablets in Linear B found on Knossos, mention, in the early form of Greek, the name of *Ke-re-te* as opposed to that of *A-ka-wi-ja-de*, thus assuming an ethnic distinction between the earlier inhabitants of Crete and the later Achaean invaders.

Miniature gold double axes from Arkalokhori dated 3000–2000 BC. Iraklion Archaeological Museum. (Author's photo, courtesy of the museum)

Proto-Hellenes

The Indo-European population migrated from Central and Northern Europe around 2000–1800 BC. These new people spread all over the Greek mainland and islands, mixing with the early Aegean inhabitants, becoming the Achaean people.

The ethnic change is confirmed by a new language. All extant forms of ancient Greek clearly derive from a common ancestor called Proto-Indo-European, a language that engendered a large number of other languages found across much of the Eurasian continent, from India to Norway. These closely related tongues show that the Indo-Europeans must have migrated over thousands of miles in different directions, settling in lands across a wide swath of the Eurasian continent. The Indo-Europeans tended to enter a region in successive waves. They rarely migrated into an area just once, and Greece was no exception. As early as 2000 BC one Indo-European contingent had begun infiltrating the Greek peninsula and by the end of that millennium at least three major discrete migrations of these intruders had surged across various parts of Greece.

EARLY CONTINENTAL AEGEAN SIEGE WARFARE, SESKLO, ABOUT 4400 BC

The scene represents the hypothetical incursion of raiders against the fortified Neolithic settlement of Sesklo. Note the house reconstruction based upon the work of the archaeologist in the Volos Museum. **(1)** The 'Pelasgian' citadel leader is brandishing a copper axe and wears a splendid example of a copper dagger inserted in leather and copper belt. Jewellery, such as earrings, necklaces and bracelets, was commonly worn as a status symbol by both genders during this period. On the leader's head is a primitive form of *pilos* cap, fitted with horns similar to those discovered in a steatite statuette of the period, probably reflecting the worship of the bull and the sacral character of the leader. **(2)** The body of this hunter-warrior is covered in tattoos in red minium, similar to those on the acrolithic statuettes of Dimini. Note the obsidian arrowheads and the primitive shape of the bow, reconstructed according to archaeological findings and graffiti. His simple but effective hide clothing was probably very common in Neolithic settlements in the Aegean region. **(3)** This man represents one of the elite warriors of the citadel who formed the bodyguard of the leader. His spear and the hypothetical reconstruction of his square shield (some scholars draw comparison with those of Middle East Sumerian culture) indicate the possibility of fighting in a pre-phalanx formation.

Copper and bronze weapons from the Cycladic islands and Crete, 2800–1900 BC. Iraklion Archaeological Museum.
a) copper leaf-shaped dagger, 2800–2300 BC from Amorgos (ECII)
b) copper leaf-shaped dagger, 2300 BC from Cyclades
c) copper leaf-shaped spearhead, 2300 BC from Cyclades
d) prepalatial dagger from Zintas, Crete.
(Author's photo, courtesy of the museum)

A   B   C   D

Important data about this migration can be deduced from the genealogies of these 'Hellenes' compiled in historic age. The most salient feature of these genealogies is that they present a conglomerate of mutually irreducible branches, each of which can be traced to its own separate origins. This heterogeneity strongly suggests that the genealogical lore of 'Hellenes' envisaged as the populations inhabiting Greece in the 2nd millennium BC did not have the same origin. The genealogies reflect an initial association of the proper Hellenes with central and northern Greece, and their subsequent infiltration into the Peloponnese, which was inhabited by the so-called descendants of Inachus and other non-Hellenic groups. The latter, in the course of time, became part of a larger body of Hellenes defined linguistically and culturally rather than on strictly tribal grounds.

The presence of newcomer princes in the genealogies could reflect therefore a major geo-political change, indicating the gradual dispersal of the Hellenic elements over the Aegean Sea. Judging by the fact that the newcomers are invariably represented as marrying into local ruling families and subsequently intermingling with them, the dispersal of the Hellenes over the Aegean region was not thought to be necessarily accompanied by violence. The archaeological and linguistic evidence partially agrees with this picture, especially with regard to the Peloponnesus. At an earlier stage, there are few breaks in the continuation of the same material culture between MH and LH periods, except for there being a more pronounced military character to their society.

The introduction of the newcomers was not always peaceful however, especially when they moved to the islands and Crete. Saeger found some evidence on Mochlos, where he came across masses of charred human bones in LM IB houses. Also, on the same island, at the beginning of LM II, attackers targeted ceremonial buildings, which were centres of Minoan worship and housed objects associated with the Minoan goddess. At that time it was in the best interest of the Achaeans to eliminate rival centres of Minoan power and any resistance to their occupation of *Ke-re-te* cosmological centres.

Achaean society was centred on warfare; its warrior elite was structured to maintain its power and government through warfare. Crete and the islands, after the gradual expansion on the mainland, were the targets of the military victories that the Achaean warrior elite required to sustain itself.

CHRONOLOGY

BC

*c.*21,000	Paleolithic man-made stone wall within a cave in Theopetra near Kalambaka on the northern edge of the Thessalian Plain.
*c.*7000–4400	Proto-ceramic/Early Neolithic settlement of Sesklo in Thessaly.
*c.*7000	Proto-ceramic/Early Neolithic settlement in the Knossos region of Crete.
*c.*4800–4500	Middle/Late Neolithic settlement of Dimini in Thessaly.
*c.*3100	Start of Bronze Age culture on mainland Greece, the Cyclades and Crete.
*c.*3100–1900	Minoan Prepalatial Period on Crete (EM I–III & MM IA).
*c.*3000–2600	Initial settlement in Troy I.
*c.*2700–2000	Organized settlements in the Cyclades.
*c.*2600–2300	Period of EM II pottery.
*c.*2500–2200	Early Bronze Age strong fortified settlement of Lerna in Argolis.
*c.*2400	Destruction of Troy II.
*c.*2000–1800	Migration from Central Europe/Asia Minor to mainland Greece.
*c.*1930	Building of the first huge labyrinth in Knossos.
*c.*1930–1700	Social and political development of the Minoan Protopalatial Period on Crete (MM IB–IIB). Destruction of most of the earlier Cretan palaces at the end of this period.
*c.*1700–1450	Minoan Neopalatial Period on Crete (MM III–LM IB). Minoan colonies formed across the Southern Aegean, from Kithera to Jasos. Building of the Minoan trading empire and thalassocracy. Trading posts established with force.
*c.*1700–1200	Troy VI established by Neo-Trojans.
*c.*1650–1550	Grave Circle B at Mycenae (LH I).
*c.*1650	Foundation of Hattusas-Bogazkoy by Hattusili I.
*c.*1628	Cataclysmic eruption of Thera (Santorini).
*c.*1600	Cyclades under Minoan influence.
*c.*1550–1425	Grave Circle A at Mycenae (LH I–IIB).
*c.*1500–1450	Zenith of the Neopalatial Cretan civilization in art and architecture; destruction of Mochlos, Achaeans at Knossos, Phaistos, Haghia Triada, Kydonia and Malia on Crete (Linear B), and the Cyclades (LM 1B–II).
Beginning of LM II (1440–1425)	Achaean rulers well established in Knossos; second destruction of Mochlos and desecration by external intruders of its important ceremonial building in the last quarter of 15th century BC.

MILITARY ORGANIZATION

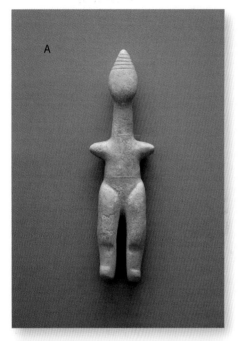

Greek mainland

Very little is known about the military organization of the first 'Greek armies' from the 9th millennium to the 3rd millennium BC, which coincides with the beginning of Cycladic civilization. The weapon finds can tell us nothing about the existence of true armies; armed groups were probably organized only on a tribal basis. As confirmed by the archaeological evidence, the first organized armies started to exist only when the various groups of nomad hunters began to settle and to farm, developing the concept of property and of social stratification, and the necessity to protect their community.

From 6000 BC more can be understood, particularly about the military tactics and weaponry of the early inhabitants of the mainland. In Sesklo (5800–4400 BC) the Greek archaeologists Tsountas and Theokaris discovered the house of a military leader at the top of the acropolis. This leader would have had his own guard, either to protect him and the acropolis or the inhabitants. Based on Theokaris' studies we can estimate the number of citizens at about 2,500–4,000 persons, the number of warriors can be calculated at around 800–1,000 men, ten per cent of whom probably formed the chief's personal guard.

The fossil remains of small horses have also been found by the archaeologist Aris Poulianos suggesting that, especially in Thessaly, these horses were tamed and raised by the first organized communities. The employment of these animals for war is however not confirmed.

Cycladic hunter-warriors

The few so far attested hunter-warrior figurines date to the end of the Early Cycladic II Period (2800–2300 BC), mainly from Syros, Naxos and Kea. Some researchers have linked their appearance with the upheavals observed in the Aegean region in this period, which were accompanied by violent destruction and the capture or abandonment of a significant number of settlements in the Aegean and Asia Minor.

The general impression given by graves and statuettes is of a society of hunter-warriors, distinguished by their social rank, at the head of villages defended by strong fortifications. The use of metal was not limited to combat but was also enveloped in symbolism. It was also used to create prestigious objects. Moreover, weapons appear to have been successively repaired, possibly as a way of preserving their connection with a glorified past or heroic individuals. Other metal objects, such as diadems and grooming utensils, need to be viewed in the light of growing emphasis on social and personal identity.

The limited number of metal objects, as well as their restricted circulation, further supports the special social standing of hunter-warriors, especially as poorly furnished

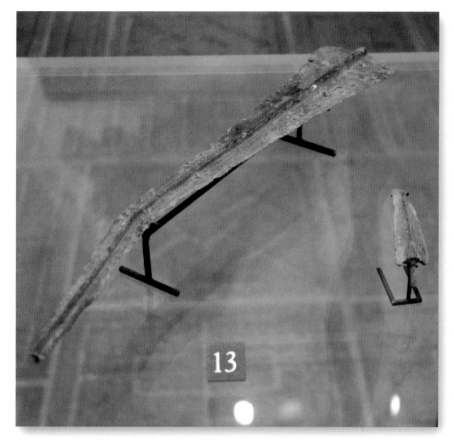

Cycladic long dagger and arrowhead, c.2700–2300 BC, from Amorgos. Found in a grave together with statuettes, the blade still showed traces of tinning. The hilt, made from perishable material, has not survived and was fixed to the blade by two rivets, one of which is still visible. Louvre Museum, Paris. (Author's collection)

graves were the norm in the Cyclades. Nevertheless, the ornate appearance of some of the weapons suggests that there may have been a thin line between actual fighting/hunting duties and the status associated with such activities. The impetus behind Cycladic warfare may have been the acquisition of prestige goods, animals or crops.

The communities of hunter-warriors were possibly formed not only by men. Some of the Cycladic hunter-warrior figurines seem to be anatomically male and female or ambiguous. On the whole, scholars entertain various possible explanations:

1) Third-gender individuals existed and could assume a special role in relation to warfare/hunting activities.

2) Sexually ambiguous hunter-warrior figurines represented mythical beings.

3) Representations of the female form and warrior insignia were compatible in the minds of the prehistoric audience, recognizing actual or mythical female hunter-warriors.

4) Women were 'transformed' into men by crossing from one gender to another, possibly in line with age, status or lineage. Alternatively, the legend of tribes of warrior women was born in this period, as in the myth of the Amazons, and we cannot exclude, in a society in which the main divinity was probably female, that women took part in war together with men.

The objects that have been found in tombs do not conclusively indicate whether both men and women were hunter-warriors. Possibly age, descent and ancestry, rather than gender, may have been the underlying criteria for distinguishing social status in the Early Bronze Age Cyclades.

Ke-re-te

The first attested civilization of Crete, the Minoan, shows us that its inhabitants were not without weapons. They deposited arms as ritual offerings in cave sanctuaries and graves, weapons that were certainly used both for war and hunting. The men are often depicted as figurines wearing daggers hanging from their belts. Nevertheless, the whole panoply of weapons and military equipment began to be available to the Minoans only shortly before the invasion of Crete by the Achaeans, and was the result of commercial exchanges between the Minoans and cities on the mainland. The first evidence of use of chariots and horses in the Aegean seems to be no earlier than LM I or LH I, also probably linked with the influence and the arrival of the warlike Achaeans.

In the ferocious world of the Bronze Age the Minoans were no different from their neighbours in their attitude to military aggression. However we do not know a lot about their military organization. Indigenous troops under local aristocratic leaders, under the nominal leadership of the princes of the main cities, formed the main military manpower, although it might also be possible to identify mercenaries, as suggested by the 'Captain of Blacks' fresco. The army was mainly infantry, fighting without the support of war chariots.

Until the occupation of Knossos by the Achaeans, the proportion of the Cretan population engaged in military service probably remained more or less constant; Crete was protected by its fleet and the vast distance of water that separated it from its neighbours. However, according to Faure and his study of Minoan art, warriors formed the second tier of Minoan society. The king was at the top of the army, but he could not be present everywhere. While the palace established military orders, the equipment used by warriors and on ships and the number of troops and their ranks, it is obvious that the recruitment, composition and movement of the units were the responsibility of the officers.

The high dignitaries held military charges and became rich with booty taken from the enemy, as well as with the income (*kama*) from the estates awarded them by the kings or princes. Aristotle said that the caste system, still present in Crete during his time, was already in existence in Minos' age, and, as in Egypt, the warriors were a class distinguished from the farm-settlers.

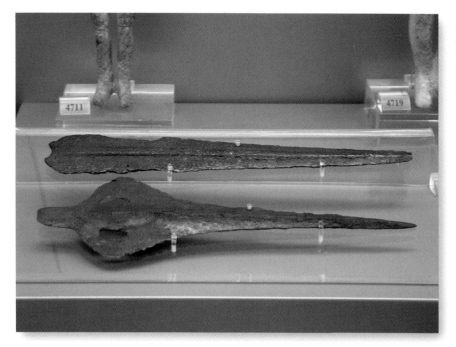

Cycladic copper dagger and spear point dated about 2200–2000 BC. Athens Archaeological Museum. (Author's photo, courtesy of the museum)

Minoan thalassocracy

The Minoans were, in the main, an important trading community throughout the Mediterranean, involved in trading tin, copper, gold, silver and ceramics. However, the vision created by Evans of a *pax Minoica* should be revised in the face of the ever-growing evidence that the Minoans engaged in major internal armed conflict and acted aggressively towards other societies.

According to the 5th-century Greek historians, the Minoans created a thalassocracy in the Aegean, the first 'maritime' empire in history. Thucydides' account acknowledges that it rests on tradition: 'Minos, according to tradition, was the first person to organize a navy. He did control the greater part of what is now the Aegean Sea; he ruled over the Cyclades, in most of which he founded the first colonies, putting his sons in as governors after having driven out the Carians. And it is reasonable to suppose that he did his best to put down piracy in order to secure his own revenues.' Herodotus has more information regarding Minos and Minoan sea power; he says that Polycrates of Samos was 'the first Greek we know of to plan a dominion of the sea, unless we count Minos of Knossos'. According to him, Crete was inhabited in ancient times by non-Greek peoples, dominated by a king called Minos of mythical origin. In the *Histories*, he describes a massive Cretan naval expedition to the town of Camicus in Sicily, which led to the destruction of the Cretan fleet in a storm, as a result of which the shipwrecked Cretans settled in Sicily, leaving Crete depopulated – after which it was settled by the Greeks (7.171f.). Furthermore, Herodotus dates Minos to three generations before the Trojan War (7.172); in other words, the mid- to late 14th century BC, which places Minos 100 years after the Greek conquest of Crete and, therefore, makes him an Achaean warlord, not a pre-Greek Minoan.

Pottery model of a dagger probably made in northern Cyprus, about 2200–2000 BC. This very interesting ceramic (red polished) model of a dagger and its decorated sheath have been found in the cemetery of *Vounous*, Cyprus. British Museum. (Author's photo, courtesy of the museum)

Cycladic hunter-warrior statuette, believed to be from Syros. The figure bears a modelled penis sheath attached to a belt. The penis sheath could be interpreted as an anatomical feature or could be viewed as male apparel worn on an anatomically female body. In a society that condoned flexibility of gender, one gender may have been deliberately associated with insignia of the other gender, especially if both participated in military and hunting practices. (Drawing by Andrea Salimbeti ex Mina)

Minoan warrior reconstruction, from a votive statuette of 2000 BC. The modelled daggers attached to male figurines from peak sanctuaries and elsewhere suggest that in Pre- and Protopalatial Periods the male warrior's social identity was defined, at least in part, by the possession and carrying of a weapon. (Drawing by Andrea Salimbeti ex Houston)

Although some scholars, such as Chester Starr, dismiss the existence of any Minoan sea empire, others try to extract historical information from the accounts of the 5th-century historians, in combination with archaeological discoveries. Thucydides' information seems very circumstantial, and the 'traditions' from which he gleaned his information both remembered the existence of a Minoan sea power and offered detail about it. Archaeology has proved that the Minoans had established a significant colonial presence in the Cyclades, just as Thucydides says. It is also clear that Minoan trade routes extended throughout the Aegean and the eastern Mediterranean. Aside from Minos' organization of the first navy and creation of an Aegean thalassocracy, Thucydides provides neither a chronological framework for his statements nor any indication of Minos' ethnicity; Minos could just as well have been a Greek ruler of Crete as a pre-Greek Minoan. The Minoan settlements on the Cyclades might not have been colonial possessions of Crete but they could equally have been independent, as were later Greek colonies. The existence of some sort of Minoan thalassocracy cannot be proved, but perhaps it seems more likely than not. Clearly, the Minoans were a seafaring people, dependent on maritime trade for raw materials, especially copper and tin, the constituent elements of bronze. They had a particular need to secure the sea routes on which goods travelled to and from their island. To protect their trade against piracy, the Minoans would have needed not just to build a navy, but also to extend their political control beyond Crete. They would have needed to deprive the pirates of bases by capturing and occupying the islands that pirates used. This could confirm Thucydides' claim about ruling over the Cyclades and 'colonizing' its islands.

B **CYCLADIC SETTLEMENT AND FORTRESS IN KASTRI-CHALANDRIANI, SYROS, ABOUT 2300 BC**

(1) The warrior is copied from a statuette from Syros. He wears a prototype Greek *pilos*, made from organic material. The spear, from Amorgos, has its point attached to the shaft by means of holes in the blade. Note the dagger from the same locality, worn inside a typical baldric in red leather, decorated in a herringbone pattern. **(2)** The design of circular and geometrical tattoos on the body of this hunter can be seen on the remains of a number of statuettes. The early bow, wood reinforced with goat's horn and sinews, is copied from a specimen represented on a mosaic from Knossos. In Cycladic graves a connection is noticeable between weapons and bone tubes, which often contained blue azurite pigments (in the Manika cemetery these are predominantly associated with female skeletons). The kind of female garment seen here worn by this priestess **(3)**, in the colours of the Dama of Phylakopi and in the tradition of coloured Aegean clothes, bears close similarity with Sumerian and Mesopotamian costumes and is also represented on an early Minoan ivory cylinder from Knossos, dated around 2100 BC. Note her rich jewels, taken from specimens from Mochlos and Archanés.

Bronze dagger with gold hilt from Crete, dated 2000–1800 BC. Iraklion Archaeological Museum. (Author's photo, courtesy of the museum)

The collapse of Minoan power

We know with certainty, both from mythology and onomastics, that many Hellenes were living in Crete even before they conquered the island. All we know for sure is that Greeks from the mainland replaced native Minoans in control of the palace at Knossos in the middle of the 15th century BC. This transition was accompanied by the destruction of the other palaces, showing that the replacement was violent. If the Minoans had command of the sea, it is hard to imagine how the Greeks could have mounted a successful invasion and conquest of Crete by launching an amphibious attack on the island. We should however remember that by now the Greeks

Votive figure from Petsophàs-Klisomeni dated 19th–17th century BC. Iraklion Archaeological Museum. (Author's photo, courtesy of the museum)

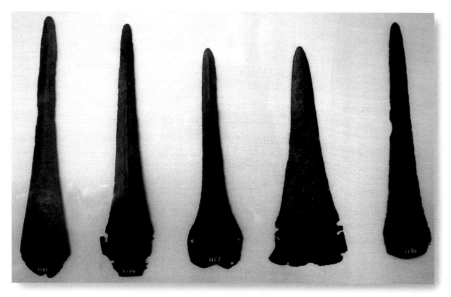

Group of Minoan bronze short swords from Iraklion and Ziba dated from 1800–1700 BC. Iraklion Archaeological Museum. (Author's photo, courtesy of the museum)

had certainly become wealthy. Mainland culture had blossomed after the eruption on Thera, with large palaces appearing at numerous locations and rich burial remains testifying to the wealth of the rulers.

We can only speculate about the way in which the Greeks came to conquer Crete. What is a matter of fact is that, as suggested by Catling, the differences between the three main LM II–LM IIIA1 cemeteries of Knossos, i.e. Zapher Papoura, Ayos Ioannis-New Hospital Site and Sellopoulo, probably reflect the mixed composition of the new Knossian ruling class between 1450 and 1380 BC. These tombs display specific Achaean features, while the cemeteries of Mavro Spelio and Gypsadhes may more convincingly be related to the Minoan community. Surprising new Achaean military graves were recently found in Khanià-Kydonia at the end of 2003, contemporary and similar to the Knossos graves and revealing a great amount of military equipment.

The occupation of Knossos also had a strong impact on the other Cretan communities in terms of military organization. It created a sudden need for soldiers, a need that could be met only by drawing from the population in the countryside. At the very time when there was a great demand for agricultural workers, the occupation required that these workers perform military service. The previous Cretan elite focused on ritual and religious matters, but now organizational skills were required with a focus on military organization and strategy. However, a possible central authority was wiped out with the occupation of Knossos, and the following Minoan collapse was the result of imbalance between the need for military personnel to counter the invaders and the need to feed a growing population. The Cretans outnumbered the Achaeans, but barbarian raiders always had certain advantages over state-organized defenders. Great mobility is one of the most important factors, since the Achaeans could come and go as they wished; they could lose many battles without losing the war, whereas the defenders of the palaces could lose only once and their palace would become a base for invaders. Fighting with superior weapons, horses and chariots, the Achaeans also had the advantage over the Minoan infantry forces. When the large supplies of food stored in the palace fell into enemy hands, Minoan Crete fell.

CLOTHING

Garments

There are no representations showing the garments used by the Aegean Neolithic people but, based on later images, we can assume they were generally naked or wearing just a small kilt to protect their genitals, although it is probable during the cold season that they could have worn simple bell-shaped skirts or capes made from sheepskin. Cycladic sculpture shows in fact that the majority of people generally went naked, with parts of the body painted in blue and red. Some hunter-warriors are represented wearing a kind of belt with a garment for genital protection, and the women sometimes wore a long decorated skirt or a flounced cloak.

Minoans wore a variety of complex coloured garments that were sewn together in very much the same way that modern garments are made; they made skirts and blouses that were shaped to the body of the wearer. The ancient Minoan men wore only loincloths, which were small pieces of fabric wrapped around the waist to cover the genitals. They were made from a wide variety of materials, such as linen, leather or thick wool, and decorated with bright colours and patterns. Many had a decorative application or sheath that covered and protected the penis, and some had long aprons in the front and back with tassels or a fringe. While early Minoan men usually went bare-chested, in the later years of Minoan civilization they often wore simple tunics and long robes. A tiny waist was prized, and both men and women wore tight belts made of metal, which held their waists in. Some scholars believe that these belts must have been worn since early childhood, forcing the waist to stop growing.

Unfortunately, very few fragments of clothing have survived Crete's temperate, damp climate. The evolution of Cretan costume during different periods of Cretan and Aegean civilization is however well documented in art.

Warriors and princes, like other men, wore a loincloth, which varied in shape according to the material used. The loincloth could be arranged like a short skirt or a double apron. It generally finished at the back in a point that was sometimes lengthened and turned up resembling an animal's tail. Another loincloth could be worn over the first, but back to front, forming a flounce

EARLY AEGEAN WARRIOR 3000–1700 BC

(1) The Cycladic princes and leaders made use of jewellery as symbols of social status. Apart from weapons, a whole range of new metal items, such as jewellery and toilet articles, also make their appearance in the Aegean Early Bronze Age, marking an emphasis on the physical body and status. Note his religious azurite skin painting and the elaborate dagger, as well as his penis sheath. **(2)** A *Ke-re-te* male warrior costume from a statuette from Kampos (Laconia). He wears a small loincloth, which would be of wool or linen, and a metal belt made of bronze or copper. The long hair is wrapped in a net or hood. He holds a typical Minoan dagger and wears high white boots. The bronze double axe was indicative of religious and political power.

Some examples of swords (Naxos, Malia, Aegina) and daggers (Cyprus, Crete, Malia) are illustrated here with a reconstruction of a hypothetical linen scabbard, restored from fragments still found attached to the blade. The pointed blade of the spears (samples come from Amorgos, Arkesine and Malia) was pierced with holes through which a cord could be threaded. This method was prevalent even at the beginning of the second millennium, having originated in Anatolia in the second half of the third millennium. In the background three different warrior heads are reconstructed from a) and b) Cretan seals and c) Phaistos disk, the last wearing a conical helmet, possibly copper.

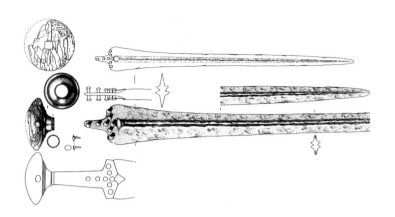

that extended to mid-thigh with two points, one each at the front and back. The men's thin waists were accentuated by cloth belts heavily decorated with metal.

Ceremonial attire consisted of a long, tunic-shaped gown made in bright colours with rich embroidery. It was reserved for princes, nobility and priests. A short cape or a cloak made from animal skin or wool was worn over the loincloth or gown for warmth. Men of any rank or status roamed freely in the nude.

A-type sword from Aegina, dated about 1700 BC. One of the earliest A-type bronze swords dated about 1700 BC is attributed to Aegina. In this interesting specimen the tang and the shoulders show eight rivets for fixing the handgrip and one rivet on top of the tang used for the upper knob. This sword is 79.1cm long. The sword-makers were conscious of the weakness of the separate handle in the early models and attempted to compensate for it by attaching a tang, an elongation of the blade, which was enclosed by the handle for extra support. (Drawing by Andrea Salimbeti ex Kilian-Dirlmeier)

Textiles

Early Minoans wore animal skins, but by 3000 BC they had mastered the art of weaving flax and, later, wool. Proof that spinning and weaving were already known in Neolithic communities is furnished by the discovery of numerous spindle weights.

Everything connected with clothing, from sheep-shearing to cutting cloth, was a domestic occupation, but dyeing was done by skilled professionals. The industry used vegetable pigments as well as the purple extracted from shellfish.

Jewellery

Many of the jewellery items that survived from the Minoan Period were found in tombs, buried with their owners. The average Minoan wore necklaces of stone, while the wealthy proudly displayed beads of blue steatite or blue paste (imitating lapis lazuli), agate, amethyst, cornelian or rock crystal, or metal plates. Mixed with these beads were pendants bearing animal, bird or human motifs. Pendants and earrings were very popular, for both men and women.

Hats and headdresses

Hats included high caps, pointed hats, berets, turbans and even tri-corns, perhaps with ritual significance, decorated with rosettes and crowned with a curled plume or ribbon. Some hats had white trimmings, others black. Minoan men wore their hair in a long wavy style.

Shoes

The main representations of Cycladic hunters show them mostly barefoot. However, we cannot exclude the possibility that footwear could have been rendered in colour on statuettes.

Cretans went barefoot indoors, but many wore shoes outside. In particular the upper class never showed themselves in public without shoes or sandals, although warriors are often represented barefoot. The shoes of high functionaries and the military elite were finely worked and attached above the ankles with thick thongs, as shown in the 'Master seal' of Khanià. Minoans' shoe types included slipper shoes, moccasin-style socks, sandals and high, closed boots for travelling. The main warrior's footwear was a white half-boot made of white leather or chamois, reaching to the calf. Their boots could also be red with thongs tied seven times round the leg.

Minoan swords from a grave in Malia, 1700–1600 BC. Other early A-type blades appear to be those from MM II Malia, produced by an established weapons workshop. These rapiers were often exported to the Greek mainland and dispersed among the warlike Achaean warlords. These swords, like all type A examples, have pronounced edges and are more similar to medieval and early-Renaissance cut-and-thrust long swords. Iraklion Archaeological Museum. (Author's photo, courtesy of the museum)

WEAPONS AND ARMOUR

During the Paleolithic Period the first weapon finds mainly consist of arrow points, spear and javelin heads made of stone. In the successive Neolithic Period the weapons did not show any substantial difference until the introduction of copper.

In contrast to Anatolia and the Near East, the earliest stages in the development of Mediterranean metallurgy appear only after about 5500 BC. During the late Neolithic Period in the Aegean (c.5500–4500 BC), copper pins turn up at Dikili Tash, Paradeissos and Kitsos Cave, while two small daggers have been recovered from Aya Marina in Phocis. It was only during the following final Neolithic Period (c.4500–3700 BC), however, that Aegean metallurgy began to flourish. Copper, gold, silver and lead artefacts have been recovered from at least 12 different sites, including large assemblages of metal finds, such as at Zas Cave on Naxos and copper daggers from Dimini and Sesklo.

The true revolution in weapon making was when, in about 4000–3000 BC, the first inhabitants of present-day Greece began to work in bronze and brass. Metal weapons appear on most of the Aegean islands a little before the middle of the 3rd millennium BC. The most common offensive weapons found were spearheads, daggers, swords and arrowheads.

Bronze tangles dagger of Type II variant A with gold hilt from Malia, dated 18th–17th century BC. Iraklion Archaeological Museum. (Author's photo, courtesy of the museum)

Detail of one of the Malia swords, 1700 BC. Note the combination of gold plating and crystal knob. The sword is the natural expansion of the broad-stemmed dagger blade with which it was associated in the grave, and had similar gold plate with the same engraved herringbone pattern decorating its hilt. Iraklion Archaeological Museum. (Author's photo, courtesy of the museum)

The mining of local metal in Neolithic settlements confirms the *in situ* development of Aegean metallurgy, contradicting earlier theories that raw materials and objects were introduced only from the East and/or the Balkans. The Aegean region was at the time one of the regions that received (via exchanges with the rest of the Neolithic world) metallurgical knowledge and developed it *in situ*. The greater importance of metal weapons is in evidence in the Aegean after the Early Bronze Age, especially with respect to 'cutting-edge' weapons of tin-alloyed copper such as long daggers with strong midribs and spearheads.

Spears and javelins

Hunting and the defence of livestock from predators are likely to have been the main purposes for which most members of the population would own a weapon.

Spears and javelins are the most common weapons used in the Aegean region. Even if no complete wooden shaft has survived, artistic representations can give a reasonable indication of the length of spears or javelins. The first can be mainly divided into long spears, in some cases probably more than 3m long, and short spears. The longer spears were used in a thrusting action, normally with both hands. The javelins were usually shorter and equipped with smaller points, and were mainly used for throwing. Based on artistic representations, Höckmann identified three types of javelin: long, short and heavy, and light for long-distance throwing.

CENTRO-EUROPEAN MIGRATION ON THE PRESENT-DAY GREEK MAINLAND ABOUT 2000–1800 BC

The plate sets out to show a group of those Indo-European peoples who migrated into Greece around 2000–1800 BC, probably from the Balkans and Central Europe. **(1–2)** The warriors in the foreground wear early forms of boar's tusk helmet copied from the Mariupol and Kolonna specimens. This very primitive boar's tusk helmet shows that this style of reinforcement and decoration was probably introduced to the Aegean world by the Indo-Europeans migrating from central and north European regions around 2000–1800 BC. Their weapons and jewellery are copied from various finds in central Greece, such as the bronze spearhead from Thiva (Thebes). **(3)** The 'proto-Greek' Mynian woman is copied from a pottery idol from Euboea. Note the early Aegean style of her garments, borrowed from Crete and the islands. **(4)** The early form of chariot is copied from a Late Neolithic pottery model dated 1700 BC from central Europe (Slovakia). The use of the chariot was most likely spread to the Greek mainland from the Near East after the Middle Bronze Age (about 1950–1550 BC) as a result of the central and eastern European migration and the Achaeans' trade contacts with those regions, although the early attestation of its use in war comes from the Mycenaean Graves A stele.

Fragments of the so-called Town mosaic from Knossos city, representing a spearman and an archer, 18th–17th century BC. Iraklion Archaeological Museum. (Author's photo, courtesy of the museum)

During the Early and Middle Bronze Age bronze spearheads are among the objects found in the graves of the early settlements such as Sesklo and Dimini. One of the earliest spear points in evidence in the Aegean region is a leaf-shaped copper specimen dated around 2700–2300 BC from the Cycladic island of Amorgos. Similar leaf-shaped spearheads, both in copper and bronze, are in evidence in several Cycladic settlements.

Elongated spear points have also been found in Cyprus in the Nikosia and Steno settlements. These blades, 15.7cm and 18cm long, date to around 2300 BC.

Other types of bronze spear and javelin points dating from around 2300–2000 BC have been recovered from Tomb 78 of the cemetery in Vounous (Cyprus). These kinds of spearheads have a tang, ending in a hook, which was fixed into the wood. The blade was then further secured to the wooden shaft by latching cord.

According to Höckmann-Snodgrass, the Group A spear and javelin points have a flat or narrow fixation tang and a blade without grooves. In some specimens the blade is pierced with two elongated holes or four small holes through which a cord could be threaded. Attested to both in Crete and on the Greek mainland, they have a length of 15.5cm up to a maximum of 38cm. They are mainly dated to the MM/MH period (about 2200–1600 BC).

The Group B spear and javelin points have a unique 'shoe' shape with a hollow clutch in which the wooden shaft was fixed. Attested to both in Crete and on the Greek mainland, they had a general length of 11cm to 18.6cm. and are mainly dated in the MM to LM IB (about 2200–1500 BC) in Crete and MH III to LH IA (about 1600–1550 BC) for the specimens found in the mainland settlements.

Group F included several types mainly attested to in Crete and in the East Aegean islands. Their blades form an acute angle with the hand-grip. It has an oval shape with a rectangular or flat central rib. The tube has the typical 'cannon' shape with a longitudinal fissure. The general length is from 17.5cm to 45cm, and they date from MM to LM/LH IIIB–C (about 2000–1100 BC).

The blade of Group G made a less acute angle with the hand-grip. It has an oval shape cross section but larger than that of Group F; also the central rib varies in shape. The typology is mainly attested to in Crete and in the Aegean islands, with a general length from 12.3cm to 45.5cm. The early specimens are dated MM–MM III (about 2000–1600 BC) with some examples dated LM–LH I (about 1550 BC).

The spear and javelin points of the Group H ('bayonet type') are characterized by a long and narrow blade with longitudinal grooves and central rib. The blade is an extension of the tube, which is faceted and fissured. Two holes for fixation pins and a metal ring are generally present in the lower part of the tube. They are in evidence in several variants coming

from Crete (Knossos Palace), mainland Greece (shorter in dimension) and Rhodes island. The general length is from 12.5cm to 57cm. Most of them are dated LM II–III A (about 1500–1370). A beautiful example of this group dated around 1500 BC has been found in Archanes, 20.3cm long and with a blade decorated with spring motifs.

The unique example of a short and heavy spear from the tholos (dome-shaped tomb) in Vapheio (dated around LH IIA), made with a wooden shaft covered by a bronze tube with spherical elements is similar to an embossed spear shaft represented in a seal from Mirabello (Crete) dated around 1600–1550 BC. The evidence suggests that this kind of bronze shaft with spherical elements probably has a Minoan origin.

The earliest representation of spears or javelins in the Aegean region date from the EM to MM I–MM II (about 2500–1700 BC), such as the images of a medium-length spear or javelin with triangular point represented on a seal stone from Crete dated from 2500 to 2200 BC. A young warrior with a long spear is also represented on a fresco from Knossos dated around MM IIIA–B. Very long spears are in evidence in the famous battle fresco from Akrotiri on Thera. This fresco was clearly painted before the destruction of the island by an earthquake followed by a volcanic eruption, which, based on the most recent analysis,

The gold knob from an A-type sword from Malia, representing an acrobat, about 1700–1600 BC. Several weapons from the Aegean, such as daggers of black bronze from Santorini, the Skopelos swords and other specimens from Knossos have finely decorated blades and pommels in ivory or gold. This knob from Malia is one of the finest examples. Iraklion Archaeological Museum. (Author's photo, courtesy of the museum)

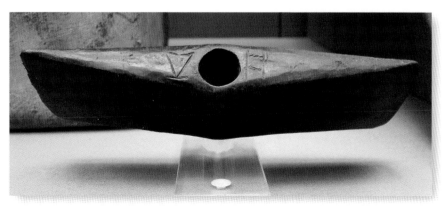

Bronze axe with two symbols in Linear A script, 1700–1450 BC, possibly from the Lasithi Plateau. The double axe was a weapon, tool and religious symbol in Minoan Crete; the Linear A shows that this specimen was probably a votive offering. London, British Museum. (Author's photo, courtesy of the museum)

Stone hammerhead, probably for ritual or ceremonial use, Minoan, 1700–1450 BC. London, British Museum. (Author's photo, courtesy of the museum)

occurred no later than 1600 BC. In the same fresco long spears are also used by some of the warriors on the ships.

It is possible that in this period the long 'naval spear' had its origin. This particular spear could have reached a length of 4m, while the common long spears normally did not exceed 2m. One or more sailor-warriors armed with such long weapons could easily strike their enemies from a safe distance. A very peculiar bronze double-headed blade, dated around 16th century BC and found at Agios Onoufrios near Phaistos (Crete), has been interpreted as a fish spear. This may have been used in conjunction with a net or on its own from an open boat, but we cannot exclude its use as a weapon.[1]

Long spears are handled by warriors or deities represented on two seal stones from Knossos dated to the end of the Middle Minoan Period (about 1600–1550 BC). On other seals from Haghia Triada and Zakros, dated around MM III/LM I (about 1550 BC), the earliest representations of active fighting with spears are shown. A warrior with a spear is also represented on a jug of bichrome wheel-made ware from Cyprus, dated about 1500 BC.[2]

Swords and daggers

One silver and two bronze Minoan daggers from Vianno and Lassithi, dated Middle Minoan Period. Iraklion Archaeological Museum. (Author's photo, courtesy of the museum)

The early swords of the Aegean Bronze Age are some of the most striking artefacts from this epoch in terms of craftsmanship and opulence. Their perceived role has at various times ranged from their being ritual objects, to their being perfectly serviceable tools of war, the early swords evolving out of the dagger. Before copper and bronze, stone was used as the primary material for cutting-edged tools and weapons. Stone is very fragile however, and therefore not practical for swords. With the introduction of copper and eventually bronze, daggers could be elongated and evolve into swords. The earliest Anatolian swords were found at Arslantepe, Turkey, dating to c.3300 BC. However sword finds are very rare up to around 2300 BC. In general during the Aegean Bronze Age, weapons with blades evolve from the dagger or knife in the Early Bronze Age to the earliest narrow-bladed 'rapier' swords, optimized for thrusting, in the Middle Bronze Age.

[1] WAR 153: *Bronze Age Greek Warrior 1600–1100 BC* (Osprey Publishing Ltd: Oxford, 2011), p. 13.
[2] WAR 153: *Bronze Age Greek Warrior 1600–1100 BC* (Osprey Publishing Ltd: Oxford, 2011), p. 5.

Pottery from Akrotiri, about 1600 BC. These vases are among the earliest representations of figure-of-eight body shields, from the same period as the famous miniature fresco. The shields seem to be hanging from a wooden lintel. They are clearly depicted with central lengthwise strips and several bosses or seams to secure the layers of hide. Iraklion Archaeological Museum. (Author's photo, courtesy of the museum)

One of the earliest swords in evidence in the Aegean region is a copper specimen from Naxos dated around 2800–2300 BC. Its design is similar to the early type of Aegean dagger. The length of this sword is 35.6cm. This kind of early leaf-shaped sword or dagger was attached to a baldric as shown on a marble statue of a hunter-warrior dated around 2300 BC from the Cycladic island of Naxos. The wooden grip was fixed to the blade by means of a tang, curved on the upper part to secure it. The scabbard was fixed by four crossed laces at the join between the two ends of the baldric.

The huge number of swords found in Crete and the various arguments put forward, by Catling, Hood, Hiller, MacDonald, Sandars and others, that many of the early Achaean swords are attributable to Minoan workshops, establishes a significant relationship between Minoan Crete and weaponry, as well as the notion of warlike Minoans. The Minoan swords considered here are limited to the time and events that led to the destruction of the Minoan palaces, but their number demonstrates that weaponry seems to have played a fundamental role in Minoan society throughout all the phases of its history. In the Neopalatial Period the sword, a tool of violence and a symbol of the warrior, was also part of the trappings of elite religious ideology.

One of the early possible representations of Minoan short swords is on a seal from Haghia Triada (Crete) dated around MM III–LM I (about 1600 BC). In this cult scene, swords and dagger blades seem to be placed with their points upwards on the altar.

The great sword was one of the most interesting inventions of the Aegean Bronze Age. Analysis of some specimens shows that the material is an alloy of copper and tin or arsenic for making bronze. When the percentage of copper or tin content is high, the bronze blades have a reddish or silver colour respectively. Whether this was done intentionally to imitate precious metals, or was simply the result of miscalculation, it is not possible to guess.

In spite of some scholars claiming that most of the Minoan weapons possessed hafts (hilts or handles) that would have prevented their use as

Aegean warriors marching in battle formation, fresco from Akrotiri, about 1600 BC. The fresco from the West House, room 5, probably represents the oldest known sea battle. A conflict and naval engagement between Aegean warriors and non-Aegean enemies (possibly Lybian pirates) seems to have taken place, and the outcome was victory for the Aegeans. The Aegean warriors arrived with their ships to protect the town and they succeeded. We see the moment of victory when they are marching on the shore in battle formation. Thera Archaeological Museum. (Author's collection)

weapons, more recent experimental testing of accurate replicas has shown this to be incorrect, as these weapons were capable of cutting flesh down to the bone (and scoring the bone's surface) without any damage to the weapons themselves.

A link between the Minoan triangular small swords or daggers and the long A-type sword (according to Sandars' classification) can be seen in the specimen found in Malia (Crete) dated around 1700 BC. This sword shows a large and long blade with a large and flat midrib. On its rounded upper part, four rivet holes are used to attach the blade to its decorated hilt and two rivet holes are present on the tang. The awesome part of this sword is its hilt, which was covered with a gold engraved plate and a marvellous crystal rock was set at the end.

Other examples of Cretan long bronze swords, which could be interpreted as ancestors of the A- and B-type swords, are attested to from the palace of Zakros.

The A-type swords made their appearance in the MM I period, continuing in use from LM I–II–III (about 1700–1600 BC) to LH I–II (about 1600–1500); the earliest of these Aegean long swords again come from the palace of Malia. Furthermore, specimens of the A-type swords are also attested to in the Cycladic and Ionian islands. These swords, a massive elongation of the dagger's design, can reach 90cm and sometimes more than 1m in length, with a strong midrib on the blade. The handle was a separate element, riveted to the blade. It has a flat narrow tang, either very short or longer with rivets. Ivory and wood decorated with gold were used for the handgrip and knob. Recent theories point to Cretan ateliers as the origin of the best specimens, including those found in the royal shafts of Mycenae.

This type of early long sword was most likely used by the warriors depicted in the Akrotiri fresco dated around 1600 BC. Behind the warriors the lower part of a long scabbard, ending with a fringed knob, is clearly visible. Another A-type sword is probably also represented in a seal from Haghia Triada in Crete, dated MM III–LM I (about 1600–1550 BC), where a warrior is using his long and narrow sword in a thrusting action. An A-type sword is probably also handled by the warrior represented in the famous 'Chieftain Cup' from Haghia Triada dated LM I (about 1550 BC).[3]

The B-type swords seem to be less common in Crete or Minoan regions, there being only a few specimens attributed to the Aegean islands. According to Dickinson, their place of origin was the Argolis. The main distinguishing feature and innovation of the B-type swords is the use of flanges, either on the shoulder of the blade itself or on the tang, i.e. the development of the full tang.

Aegean warrior, detail of a fresco from the West House, Akrotiri, about 1600 BC, Thera Archaeological Museum. (Author's collection)

The first appearance of these flanges is of the greatest importance in the history of Aegean swords. From the Aegean itself the earliest approximately datable shoulder flange is to be found on the dagger or short sword from the annexe to the smaller tholos at Haghia Triada, which is dated by Evans to MM II, possibly IIA.

Interesting B-type swords, 33cm long and 34cm long, have been found in Agioi Theodoroi (Crete) and in Kameiros (Rhodes). A B-type sword inside its scabbard is probably also represented on a stone relief from Phaistos (Crete), dated 16th century BC.[4]

From A- and B-type evolved the C-type sword, characterized by a thin blade with an abrupt rib and long flanged lateral 'horned' hand-guard turned upward. Some examples are around a metre in length. The C-type is subdivided into two groups, Ci and Cii, both very similar and used in the same period. The C-type sword measured 60–90cm (Ci) and 60–70cm (Cii), and the earlier specimens are dated from LM–LH II (about 1500 BC).

Dated from the same period as the C-type is the Di-type sword. These weapons, also known as 'cross swords' have an average length of 60–70cm and were characterized by a small horizontal cross guard. Some specimens are attributed to Crete and other Aegean islands starting from 1450 BC, so it is not clear if this type of sword has been imported

Conical horned helmets represented in Minoan linear signs on inscribed clay bars from *Malia*, *c*.1600 BC, ex Evans, 1935. Early headpieces of Cretan warriors were of leather or padded material, with horizontal ridges. (Author's collection)

[3] ELI 130: *The Mycenaeans c.1650–1100 BC* (Osprey Publishing Ltd: Oxford, 2005), p. 3.
[4] WAR 153: *Bronze Age Greek Warrior 1600–1100 BC* (Osprey Publishing Ltd: Oxford, 2011), p. 14.

Rhyton with boxers from Haghia Triada, dated 1600 BC. Iraklion Archaeological Museum. (Author's photo, courtesy of the museum)

into these regions during the considerable expansion of the mainland Achaeans or if they were already used by the Minoans. MacDonald, however, following the suggestion of Sandars and Catling, attributed it to Knossian workshops.

Some of the early Aegean triangular daggers, dated around 5500–4500 BC, have been unearthed in Ayia Marina-Phocis, Alepotrypa and Ayios Dimitrios-Triphylia, and elongated copper daggers dated around 4800–3300 BC have been found in Dimini and Sesklo.

There is always difficulty in distinguishing between short swords (dirks) and daggers, since most probably they served the same purpose. The main criterion used by scholars is the length of these weapons, but there is still no general agreement about the dividing line between the two. Because the arbitrary division of dirks and daggers on the basis of their length produces anomalies and confusion, some scholars, such as Dr Thanasis J. Papadopoulos, have decided to classify as daggers all those weapons whose general outline corresponds to the basic, standard type of dagger, paying less attention to their length, which in any case never exceeds 45cm.

Several specimens of copper leaf-shaped daggers dated EC II (about 2800–2300 BC) are attested to the Cyclades (Naxos and Amorgos) and Crete. Also, this kind of early leaf-shaped dagger was attached to a baldric or to a waist belt as in the above-mentioned marble statue of the warrior from Naxos and the Minoan statuettes from Petsofà, dated around 2300 BC.

The Minoan daggers show quite a variety, which is certainly due to the wide range of their provenance, the change in style during the period and the personal taste of the maker and the owner. Their study can help to establish some parameters of functionality.

The usual Early Minoan triangular dagger had a narrow midrib, and this was adopted on the slenderer, longer daggers of the Middle Minoan Period,

 RETURN FROM VICTORY: 'KRETES' WARRIORS WITH LYBIAN PRISONERS IN AKROTIRI, 1600 BC

All the figures are based on the Santorini frescos. **(1–2)** The Akrotiri warriors' boar's tusk helmets have a horsetail and seem to be decorated at the front and back with unidentified items, probably feathers. The throat strap is also visible. Note the huge tower shields and long spears, used in closed proto-phalanx formation. **(3)** The tattooed 'Lybian' prisoners represented in the frescos have been deprived of their main weapons, their bows and arrows being held by the guards. Note the leather quiver of one of the prisoners, worn across the shoulders of one of the soldiers. **(4–5)** Minoan women wore skirts that flared out from the waist in a bell shape, with many decorations attached to the cloth. Later designs were made from strips of fabric, sewn in ways that created rows of ruffles from waist to ankle. Women also wore close-fitting blouses that were cut low in the front to expose the breasts. Because the figure of the Minoan woman, with large breasts, large hips and tiny waist, was very similar to the female shape in fashion during the late 1800s, some scholars believe that Minoan women must have also worn some sort of framework under their skirts to support the bell shape.

Ivory vase with bull-hunting scene from Crete dated 1600–1450 BC. Iraklion Archaeological Museum. (Author's photo, courtesy of the museum)

which are best known from the collective tombs of the Messara in southern Crete. They are usually double-bladed, mostly measuring between 10 and 20cm in length, and a separate handle, made of wood, bone or ivory was attached to the blade. They varied from 11cm to 22cm, with the majority around 20cm. Some have silver rivets. The blades are relatively flat and the longer examples have a thickened midrib to prevent bending. Particularly relevant is a tangled dagger from Platanos Tholos B, with a sharp distinct midrib, round or angular, a long tapering blade and a separate hilt attached either by two rivets, set rather low in the blade on either side of the midrib, or by two pairs of rivets, one above the other. It is interesting to note that, according to Branigan, long daggers are the most common bronze artefacts of the EM–MM periods, followed by triangular daggers. This can be a useful way to calculate a warrior's burial date in the Prepalatial Period (usually one man per dagger in Messara tholoi).

The I-type dagger is represented by some late Middle Bronze Age and early Late Bronze Age daggers, which are short, tapering or leaf-shaped, usually not much more than 20cm in length and about 5.5cm in width. Their main and common characteristics are the absence of a tang (tangles) and the broad blade. Other basic features are the tapering or leap-shaped blades, with or without a midrib, bevelled edges and massive, mostly gold- or silver-plated rivets, which range in number from two to four. According to their profile, two main variants can be distinguished: A tangles flat or slightly thickened daggers (mostly tapering) and B tangles midrib daggers (mostly leaf-shaped). Some examples of these daggers dated around the 18th–17th century have been found in Haghia Triada and Malia.

Another type of dagger in evidence in Crete belongs to type II Variant A. These longer daggers vary in length between 23.6 and 43cm, most of them falling into the range of 28 35cm, with an average width of 6cm. They are characterized by elongated triangular 'winged' blades (usually having slightly flanged shoulders) with or without midrib and bevelled edges. In the butt are four massive or small rivets, either silver or gold plated or plain. Sometimes there are extra rivets and even a short tang to strengthen the handle attachments.

Horned daggers are, like tanged daggers, relatively rare, comprising very few specimens. So far, all have been found in tombs and are more or less well preserved. Size varies considerably, their lengths ranging from 26.4 to 39.5cm and their widths from 6.3 to 8cm. They differ also in general outline, but what all have in common are the generally up-drawn or horned flanged shoulders. Other essential characteristics are the relatively long and broad tang, usually with shallow or deep flanges, and the triangular blade with or without sharp distinct midribs. These daggers show similarity with the Type Cii swords. According to the shape of blade, two main variants are distinguishable: A triangular and B elongate triangular.

The cruciform dagger type comprises relatively long specimens, averaging in length between 30 and 40cm or even less and in breadth between 4 and 6cm. Their technique and shape are fairly uniform, with only minor variations. The common and basic characteristic of all these daggers, from which they take the name 'cruciform', is the protruding shoulder, which is lobed, round or angular. Other essential features are the grip, with or without a T-shaped pommel, and the pointed blade, U-shaped or tapering towards the point. Pommel, grip and shoulder are generally flanged and the flange is drawn down towards the blade, which is usually flat or flattish and plain, and only rarely ribbed or grooved. According to the above-mentioned variants in the shape of the shoulder, grip and blade, these daggers can be divided into the variants A, B, C, D and E. Some examples of variant A and B, dated around 1600 BC, have been found in Haghia Triada. Sometimes wrongly identified as daggers are the copper and bronze razors, leaf-shaped with a round blade and used for general purposes. These razors in various dimensions are in evidence throughout the Aegean region since the Cycladic Period.

Slings

Sling stones, mainly in obsidian, are in evidence in the Aegean region since the Neolithic and Early Bronze age, both on the Greek mainland and in the Cycladic islands. The primitive slings were more likely made from animal hair. The obsidian stones, accurately polished, were effective against human flesh, but less so against armour or corselet.

Other projectiles were made of limestone or unfired clay, like the Neolithic examples from Thessaly. The limestone projectiles were adequately smoothed and shaped. Through impact with the hard ground the sling stones broke apart, having a similar effect to modern hand grenades.

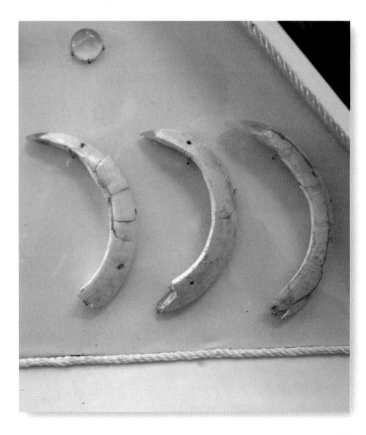

Boars' tusks for a helmet from a chamber tomb near Poros (Iraklion), dated 17th–16th century BC. Iraklion Archaeological Museum. (Author's photo, courtesy of the museum)

Axes and maces

Battle axes and hatchets are in evidence in several Aegean settlements since the Neolithic and Early Bronze Age on the Greek mainland, Cycladic islands and Anatolian coastal sites. Battle axes appear mostly in the northern Aegean, whereas maces with stone heads are also common in central and southern Greece. Some well-preserved copper axes of the Final Neolithic Period (c.4500–3300 BC) have been found in Sesklo. Two of them were found together in the centre of the acropolis beside a house wall. They were cast in moulds from 99 per cent pure copper then hammered. Their different sizes show that they came from different moulds.

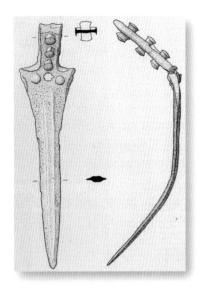

Bronze horned dagger of Variant B with bent blade from Cyprus, length 30cm. This object is dated around 1550 BC and may be considered the earliest known Aegean weapon from Late Bronze Age Cyprus. (Drawing by Andrea Salimbeti ex Karageorghis)

Other early examples of these weapons and tools were made of stone similar to some that came from Troy. These specimens were found by Schliemann during his excavations in the lower level of Hisarlik Hill, and more likely in the Troy I remains dated around 2900–2450 BC.

Copper axes or similar objects have also been found in the Cycladic islands, for instance some axes of the Keros-Syros culture, which are made of arsenical copper and dated around 2700–2200 BC. These specimens show the remarkable advances in metalwork in the Keros-Syros culture. The heavy-duty shaft-hole axes in this group were perhaps used for felling trees and stripping branches, the large flat axes for splitting tree-trunks into planks and the chisels for finer work.

A bronze axe from a grave in Lemba (Cyprus, Paphos region) dates from the early phase of the Early Bronze Age (2500–2400 BC), a period of significant change in the material culture of Cyprus, possibly related to small-scale migrations from south-western Anatolia. Metal axes bear clear evidence of the introduction of copper technology on the island. They appear at the same time as the pottery style that is associated with the so-called Philia culture.

A probable battle axe is also one of the symbols of the still-undeciphered disc from Phaistos dated 2000–1700 BC. The typical Minoan bronze double axe with a crescent-shaped blade symbol is in evidence since the first palace period like the example shown in a cretule seal from Phaistos dated around MM IIB. The Linear A inscription perhaps shows that this example was a votive offering. The double axe served as a tool, a weapon and one of the main religious symbols in Minoan Crete. It was as significant and as important in Minoan religious practice as the other two cult objects, the ritual horn and the pillar.

The earliest examples of the double-bladed axe as yet discovered in Crete belong to about the middle of the Early Minoan Age. One is a small copper axe from a tomb on Mochlos. Miniature double-bladed axes, each with a perforation at the end of its handle like that in the single-bladed Neolithic axe, have also been found. Since they are too large to be worn as amulets, they may have been intended as votive offerings, to be suspended from a shrine or from the wall of a tomb. Several miniature gold votive double axes have been found in the Arkalochori Cave in Crete (a ritual deposit, according to Kilian-Dirlmeier), dated to the 2nd millennium BC in the Second Palace Period. Votive bronze double axes, reminiscent of these gold examples, were also found in the Diktaian Cave among other gifts or offerings.

One of the most famous Minoan votive double axes excavated in the Arkalochori cave by Spyridon Marinatos is notable for being engraved with 15 symbols. Some of the symbols may be identified as Linear A characters, while others are reminiscent of those found on the Phaistos Disc. In particular, the 'Mohican' glyph (D02), which is the most frequent character on the Phaistos Disc, appears on the axe inscription both in profile and face on.

Several examples of bronze maces or hammers are in evidence in the Bronze Age excavation sites both on the Greek mainland and Aegean regions, for example Loutraki (Crete) or Haghia Triada. Examples of stone hammers in different shapes and dimensions have been found in several Aegean settlements as well as in Cyprus. These were made of different kinds of stone, such as sandstone and limestone.

Bows and arrows

In Greece the bow is likely to be acknowledged as an indigenous weapon from the Neolithic Period, even if it never equalled the importance and diffusion that bows generally had in oriental societies. From the Aegean Bronze Age two main types of bow are known: the simple wooden bow (sometimes reinforced with sinew glued to the back to prevent breakage and to increase the bow's cast) and the composite bow, which combines four materials – wood, sections of animal horn, animal tendons and sinews, and glue.

Early evidence of bows in the Aegean region is found in a seal with engraved hieroglyphic inscriptions from Malia dated around 2500 BC, where a double-convex bow and an arrow are well represented.

A hunter, armed with a simple curved bow, and his dog are depicted on a seal from Crete dated around 2200 BC. A probable composite double-convex bow is also one of the symbols on the disc of Phaistos. This type of bow seems to be different from those depicted in contemporary Aegean art so it could be a representation of a Near Eastern composite bow. A strange 'glove-like' symbol on the Phaistos disc has been interpreted by some scholars as a possible protective device used by bowmen.

In scenes from the 'Town mosaic' from Knossos dated around 1700 BC, several armed figures are depicted. Some of these warriors have been interpreted as being armed with bows and simple or double-convex bows are also represented. On a seal from Haghia Triada dated MM IIIB–LM I (around 1600–1500 BC) a male figure or a deity with a composite double-concave bow is depicted.

A large quantity of flint and obsidian arrowheads is in evidence in the Aegean region from the Neolithic Period. Most of these arrowheads have been found in the Thessaly settlements and in other regions of northern Greece. During the later period of 2500–1500 BC this early style of arrowhead was still used in several regions of the Greek mainland, Cyclades and in Crete.

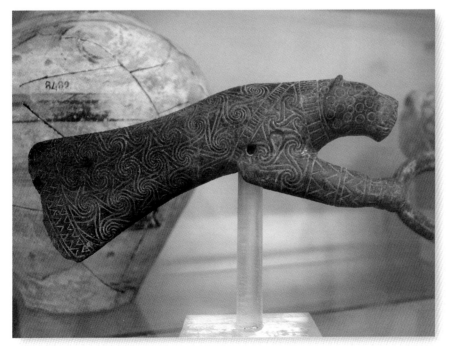

Minoan stone axe in the shape of a leopard, c. 1500 BC, from Malia, Crete. This very interesting and highly decorated axe and other weapons were clearly prestige or status weapons. They constituted powerful regalia and also imply the use of force in establishing relationships and a warlike mentality. Ceremonial maces and hammers have also been recovered from Aegina, Knossos, Zakros Palace, Haghia Triada, Palaikastro, Tylissos and Koumasa. Iraklion Archaeological Museum. (Author's collection)

Furthermore it is similar to specimens from the Balkans and central Europe from a region extending as far as the southern lands of Russia.

The flint and obsidian arrowheads in the typical 'heart' shape are in evidence from the LH I and LM I periods (about 1550 BC). These heart-shaped examples developed as an improvement on the early arrowheads in the shape of a triangle with a short tail end.

A quite large bronze arrowhead dated around 2300 BC is also in evidence from the Cycladic island of Amorgos. The shafts of the arrows have not been preserved but some tombs and deposits have yielded arrowheads and a very large deposit of thousands of arrowheads was found in the arsenal at Knossos. Bronze V-shaped arrowheads with tangs, dated around 1500 BC, have been found there. The metal variant of the tanged and recessed-based arrowheads were simply cut from bronze plate.

Bronze-cast arrowheads in the shape of a long triangle with thin tail end were discovered in the graves in Sanatorium (Crete) also dated around 1500 BC. Unlike the simple V-shaped arrowheads this type had to be cast in special moulds. Now, similar arrowheads have been found in the recently excavated Kydonia graves. Some bronze-cast arrowheads (with sockets) are also in evidence from Phaistos. This type seems to have been significantly less numerous than the V-shaped variety, perhaps for economic reasons. Some scholars believed that this and the other cast arrowheads probably have oriental origins, although they were more likely to have been manufactured in the Aegean region.

Shields

Somewhat surprising is the scarcity of defensive weapons such as shields, helmets and armour in the archaeological records. This is due to two main reasons: the partial use of perishable material such as leather, linen and other padding, and to the fact that burial rites did not usually include this type of equipment.

We do not have any evidence of the employment of shields during the Neolithic Period. If they did exist, they were probably made of organic material,

Fragment of a fresco from the Palace of Knossos representing warriors, 16th century BC. Some small isolated pieces, depicting the upper outlines of serried ranks of warriors, show soldiers hurling javelins upwards, against the enemy battlements above. The javelins are painted orange, the warriors' heads show well-defined curved crests of hair, and they wear a kind of necklace and torque. Iraklion Archaeological Museum. (Author's collection)

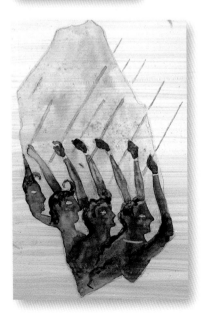

i.e. a wooden core covered with animal skin. From some scarce evidence found in Epirus and Micro-Asiatic Greece, we can suppose that the first Greek armies were equipped with shields and some kind of body protection.

One of the most common types of early Aegean body shield was the so-called 'tower shield'. It is represented mainly on wall paintings and seals. This shield was probably composed of an internal wooden structure fastened to form a cross. Several layers of toughened bull's hide were glued and stitched to a wicker structure. A rim, probably made of leather or bronze, was normally placed around the shield. Based on some representations, we cannot exclude the possibility that some shields were covered with a thin embossed or decorated bronze plate. The internal grip and baldric were used by the warrior to handle the shield properly.

The earliest evidence of the large rectangular 'tower shield' is on a fresco from Akrotiri on Thera. This kind of shield seems to have consisted of goat hide, as the skin of goats shown in the same fresco are depicted with the same colour pattern as the shield's surface. A tower shield with an upper double edge is represented on a seal from Zakros (Crete) dated around LM II (about 1500–1450 BC). In this seal a figure-of-eight shield and a helmet are also recognizable.

The figure-of-eight shield, represented on pottery, wall paintings and sculpture, both as a defensive weapon and decorative motif or cult symbol, was the other common type of Aegean body shield. Its construction was probably the same as the previous tower type, but it was formed by two internal bow-shaped pieces of wood fastened to form a cross. Longitudinal central reinforcement of bronze, tin or wood was sometimes added.

A group of approximately 150 staples in copper have been found in Tomb V at the New Hospital site at Knossos. The excavators believed these staples probably fastened the body shield oxhide layers to each other or to its wooden frame. These wires, used on both types of body shield, are some of the few examples left of perishable material from body shields used at that time. The tombs of Ayios Ioannis and the New Hospital site belonged to the newly arrived Achaeans, but the structure of the shield was virtually the same for all Aegeans.

The earliest representations of figure-of-eight body shields are present in pottery from Akrotiri. Similar shields in dark colours with white spots are depicted in a vase from Knossos dated from the LM IB. In a couple of seal stones from Haghia Triada and Knossos, dated between LM IB and LM II (about 1550–1500 BC), the use of figure-of-eight body shields is also well documented.

Fragment of a fresco from Knossos representing a naval chieftain, 16th century BC. A separate figure of a youthful warrior resting his left arm on a spear has long locks of hair, which fall over both shoulders, and his arm is raised as though he were an officer giving commands to his troops. In some respects his attitude resembles that of the young prince on the Haghia Triada cup. Iraklion Archaeological Museum. (Author's collection)

Seal stones from Kydonia (right) and unknown provenance (left), *c.*16th century BC, ex Evans, 1935. (Author's collection)

Another type of body shield used in the Aegean region is the circular or oval one with two cuts on both sides that allow better use of the shield during fighting with sword and spear. This shield, sometimes wrongly confused with the figure-of-eight shield, was later used during the Geometric and Archaic periods and it was generally known by the archaeologists as the 'Dipylon shield'.

The earliest representations of this proto-Dipylon shield are visible on a gold ring, which is part of the 'treasure of Aigina' from Crete – probably dated around TM I (about 1550 BC) – and also on a pendant from Crete, probably dated TM II (1500 BC).

Jug of bichrome wheel-made ware, decorated with armed warriors from Tomb 80 at Enkomi, Cyprus, 16th century BC. British Museum. (Author's photo, courtesy of the museum)

Helmets

The earliest representation of possible helmets or caps, probably decorated with horns, is in evidence on the Greek mainland in the Neolithic Period on two stone amulets from Sesklo dated between 5300 and 4500 BC. This kind of conical cap or early helmet was most likely made of leather with long decorative horns.

Other possible evidence of Aegean helmets is also present in Early Cycladic culture. On some male marble figures dated between 3200–2800 BC from Plastiras and Louros, horizontally ribbed, conical-shaped caps are represented, which are probably to be understood as helmets, most likely made of leather, cord or linen.

A conical-shaped helmet more likely made of copper or bronze is probably represented in one of the symbols of the famous Phaistos Disc dated 2000–1700 BC.

Remains of the crests of Trojan helmets, probably dating from around 2000 BC, were found by Heinrich Schliemann in one of the rooms of the palace in the Hisarlik Hill settlement. Because of the close commercial trade between the Anatolian and the Aegean populations, these pieces are worth mentioning as elements of the early type of East Mediterranean helmet.

Boars' tusks, probably used as reinforcement or decoration on a cap-helmet, dated around 2000 BC, have been found in Mariupol (Ukraine). It is possible that from this helmet the boar's tusk helmet found in the shaft grave of Aegina (Kolonna) dated around 1800 BC[5] developed, which is probably the departure point of the typical Achaean and Minoan boar's tusk helmets.

We know the boar's tusk helmet best from a Middle Helladic context, but this may be due to the considerable differences between Helladic and Minoan burial customs and the fact that all our evidence for Minoan helmets comes from settlements and sanctuaries, not from burials as for LH I. Worked boars' tusks, probably intended for a helmet, have been found in an LM IA tomb at Poros near Heraklion, and other pierced boars' tusks for helmets came from Kea in LM I.

Boar's tusk helmets are worn by the warriors depicted in the fresco from Akrotiri on Thera, dated around 1600 BC. Similar helmets seem also to be represented in another part of the same fresco. In the so-called 'Naval Festival' one ship seems equipped with boar's tusk helmets hanging from the passengers' cabin. A very interesting and elaborate boar's tusk helmet with large cheek guards and neck protection also covered with boars' tusks is depicted in another fresco fragment from Akrotiri dated around 1600 BC.

Conical horned helmets are represented in some Minoan linear signs, which, in a semi-pictorial form, already appear on inscribed clay bars from Malia, going back to the earliest phase of MM III (about 1600 BC). These representations already show traces of the chinstraps, and the rows of boars' tusks have left their mark in one of the representations.

A boar's tusk helmet with a large circular crest is visible on a rhyton fragment from Knossos dated around MM IIIB–LM I (about 1600–1550 BC). In particular, this type of Cretan boar's tusk helmet was also equipped with large neck and cheek guard, probably made of leather or bronze.

Interesting helmets with cheek and neck guards are represented on a vase from Katsamba (Crete) dated LM II (about 1500 BC). An ivory relief from Phaistos from the 16th century BC represents a conical helmet with small cheek and neck guards. Also in this case the reinforcement discs were probably made of ivory or metal.[6]

High conical helmets with a lower padded edge are shown in seals from Knossos dated MM III (about 1600 BC), from Zakros and Haghia Triada, as well as in a bronze figure from Iraklion dated around LH I (about 1550 BC).

On a famous rhyton from Haghia Triada dated LM I, three boxers are represented with low-profile 'hollow-eyed' helmets with long curved cheek guards and ear openings. Even if the helmets used in this boxing scene were

Minoan archer from Knossos, dated 1500 BC, from the north-east corner of the Palace Site. The archer is apparently disembarking from a boat, the horizontal edge of which is visible, and mounting rocks of conventional, scale-shaped appearance. Iraklion Archaeological Museum. (Author's photo, courtesy of the museum)

Helmets with cheek and neck guards painted on a vase from Katsamba, Crete, dated around LM II (about 1500 BC). These helmets were probably reinforced and decorated with rows of boars' tusks and small rosettes, which could have been made of ivory or metal. The upper knob with its horsetail is also visible. Iraklion Archaeological Museum. (Author's collection)

[5] WAR 153: *Bronze Age Greek Warrior 1600–1100 BC* (Osprey Publishing Ltd: Oxford, 2011), p. 23.
[6] WAR 153: *Bronze Age Greek Warrior 1600–1100 BC* (Osprey Publishing Ltd: Oxford, 2011), p. 24.

more likely made of leather or other perishable material, because of their general design we cannot exclude the possibility that bronze versions of similar helmets might have also been used in warfare. Low-profile 'hollow-eyed' helmets seem also to be represented on a seal fragment from *Zakros* dated around MM III. They are the precursors of a similar helmet visible in Late Achaean jewellery from Pilos.

Another very common type of helmet, more likely made of leather or felt and taking the form of a hood of thick padding sewn together at intervals, was the conical 'beehive' style helmet with concentric bands. Different variants of these helmets have been identified, with or without cheek and neck guards. In some cases a knob on the top, a horsetail and crest were present as well as horns. These helmets have been attested to both in Crete and on the Greek mainland. Two seals from Zakro dated around LM I (about 1550) show the simplest variant of these helmets, probably representing an 'eagle-lady' deity. A similar simple conical padded helmet seems to be depicted in a seal from Knossos dated around MM III. It is fitted with two small horns (most likely deer's horns) as decoration.

The tholos in Kephala dated LM I (about 1550 BC) revealed a fragment from an ivory plaque, with a highly interesting relief depicting two helmets. One of these helmets seems to be padded or covered with boars' tusks. The other, mostly covered with what is possibly a large body shield, has a tube at the top with plumes.

Probably from Crete, there is also a seal representing some weapons and a helmet with conical padded bands and two upper curved crests or horns. This find is most likely from the last Palatial Period.

Minoan clay seal from Kydonia, dated about 1500 BC, representing Poseidon-Poteidan commanding the sea from a coastal temple or town. Khanià Archaeological Museum. (Author's photo, courtesy of the museum)

Figure-of-eight shield, with dark background and white spots, on a vase from Knossos, dated around the LM IB (about 1500 BC). The shield seems to be hanging from a wooden lintel depicted around the vase's collar by two dark lines with several dots between, simulating the cross ridgepoles. Iraklion Archaeological Museum. (Author's collection)

Body armour

The evidence of body protection for the early Aegean warrior is very scarce and no protective or defensive weapons survive. Indeed protective garments made of animal hide or linen may have been used during warfare and hunting activity.

The outfit represented on a seal from Haghia Triada dated MM III–LM I (about 1600 BC) has been interpreted by some scholars as a possible quilted or metal-reinforced corselet made of linen, with a protective belt and lower *pteryges*-style fringes worn over a 'large *kiton*'. This interpretation is questionable and most of the scholars believe that the strange outfit is instead

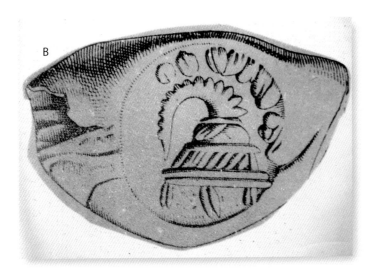

B

C

the garment worn by a priest during a cult ritual. In fact this garment shows closer similarity to that worn by the leader of the procession in the famous Harvester Vase from Haghia Triada, dated around 1550–1500 BC.

Other possible evidence of body protection is present on a steatite relief from Knossos dated from the 16th century BC, where a bowman is shown in action with vertical lines on his chest, which may represent a corselet probably made of thick stripes of cloth, while the lower part of the legs seem to be covered by some kind of greaves. However, the general

A

interpretation is that the warrior is simply naked with short trousers and that the lines are just the stylization of his muscles. If its identification as a corselet is correct, it could be a kind of poncho that allows free movement leaving the sides open. This interpretation could be confirmed by a type of non-metallic corselet with a belt and strange fringes represented on a bichrome wheel-made jug from Cyprus, dated about 1500 BC.[7] This armour seems be worn like a poncho, although its aesthetical appearance is different from the striped armour of the Cretan archer.

The high-resistance property of the boars' tusks has suggested to some archaeologists that they could also be used for reinforcing organic corselets (see the plate on page 25). This hypothesis has been formulated for the boars' tusks found in the warrior grave in Aegina dated around 1700 BC, although they are now generally accepted as elements of a prototype boar's tusk helmet because of their shape and small dimensions.

Five round bronze plates dated around 1500 BC have been found in Arkalochori. Their size and the presence of small, barely visible holes all around the plate's edge support the hypothesis that they were used on a corselet made of perishable material.[8]

Towards the end of the period in question the influence of the warlike Achaeans began to spread the use of more complete forms of armour in Crete. Two fragments of copper trapezoidal plates (48mm x 35mm and

Selection of seals from Crete, MMIII:
a) from Knossos: on this seal stone (end of the Middle Minoan Period – about 1600–1550 BC) the warrior or deity wears a rectangular shield. Because of its small size this shield cannot be considered a body shield, indeed it seems to be a short version of the tower shield used during the same period.
b) from Haghia Triada: on this seal stone, first dated by Borchhardt as MM III (about 1600 BC) but more likely dated at the destruction level of LM IB (about 1450 BC) by Wiener, a possible Minoan boar's tusk helmet is represented. This helmet shows a large curved crest and some pendants around the lower edge.
c) Warrior deity with conical cap holding long spear from Knossos (c.1600–1550 BC). (Author's collection)

---

[7] WAR 153: *Bronze Age Greek Warrior 1600–1100 BC* (Osprey Publishing Ltd: Oxford, 2011), p. 5.
[8] WAR 153: *Bronze Age Greek Warrior 1600–1100 BC* (Osprey Publishing Ltd: Oxford, 2011), p. 34.

Selection of seals from Crete, LM IA–IIB:

a) from Haghia Triada: on this seal stone, dated LM II (about 1500 BC), the warrior on the right seems to be equipped with a spear and a rectangular body shield. The shield's double edge is well represented. Two small lines on the upper part of the shaft have been interpreted as the elements used to fix the spear point into the shaft. Similar elements are in fact also represented on the spears of the Thera fresco and in at least two other pottery fragments.

b) from Zakros: the seal, dated LM IA or LM IB, represents a strange deity with equine head and a helmet with conical bands and horsetail.

c) from Zakros.

d) from Haghia Triada: on this seal, probably from the last palatial period, a warrior – armed with spear, shield and helmet (with conical bands and long horsetail) – is placed between two figure-of-eight shields.

e) from Haghia Triada: conical helmets with cheek guards, but in this case equipped with large crest and plumes, are depicted in this seal dated LM IA or LM IB.

f) from unknown site (Crete). (Author's collection)

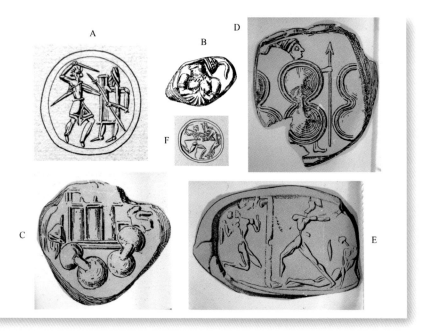

50mm x 42mm respectively), with holes around the edges and traces of quadruple linen or hemp thread that fastened the copper to a linen backing, have been found in the Tombe dei Nobili of Phaistos dated LH IIB. From the same tomb there is another copper plate fragment (295mm x 120mm) also with small holes for sewing the metal to some sort of backing, which appears to belong to a cuirass. These elements have been variously interpreted as belts, breast protection or parts of *mitra*. A fictile statue from Khanià near Gortina, dated shortly before the destruction of the Cretan palaces, seems also to represent a warrior equipped with a rigid bell-shaped cuirass fitted with a trimmed edge. The shape of the armour finds clear analogies with the breastplate of the Dendra armour in Argolis and with the small stone vessel in the shape of a cuirass from the grave of the silver and golden cup in Knossos.[9]

[9] WAR 153: *Bronze Age Greek Warrior 1600–1100 BC* (Osprey Publishing Ltd: Oxford, 2011), p. 31.

 THE MINOAN THALASSOCRACY: BOARDING OF PIRATE SHIPS IN THE AEGEAN SEA, *c.*1500 BC

The scene represents a 'cleaning up' operation in the Aegean Sea by a Minoan warship against pirates. Because of the intensive commercial trade between the Aegean population and the Near Eastern Kingdoms, some of the early Aegean ships show several similarities in general shape and design with the Egyptian ships of the same period, which is clearly shown on a large Aegean vase dated around 1700 BC.

The naval chieftain and the warriors of the Cretan ship are based on some fragments of fresco from Knossos. The Minoan ship is based on the Akrotiri fresco. The large Minoan ships were probably manned by a crew of 42–46 oars and one steering oar. Any ship, even though not properly destined for warfare, was most likely equipped with weapons for use by the crew or passengers in case of attack by hostile populations or pirates. Note, on the ship, the flat projection extending outwards from the stern just above the waterline. Interestingly, these illustrations seem to indicate the feature was added to the hull. The captain's cabin consists of wooden poles wrapped in oxhide, sometimes decorated with religious symbols both Aegean and Egyptian. These cabins were probably portable so they could be moved on and off the ships.

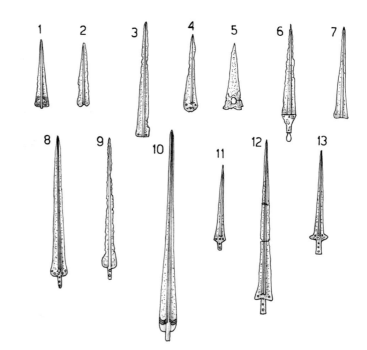

Selection of early Aegean swords. Aegean sword types are dependent on analysis of the hilt and handle. (Drawing by Andrea Salimbeti)
1) 2800–2300 BC from Naxos
2) 2500 BC from Naxos
3) 2000 BC from Amorgos
4) 1800 BC from Iraklion
5) 1800 BC from Ziba
6) 1700 BC from Malia
7) 1700 BC from Zakros
8) 1700 BC from Aegina
9) 1700 BC from Malia
10) 1700 BC from Arkalochori
11) 1600 BC from Hagioi Theodori
12) 1450 BC from Knossos
13) 1450 BC from Knossos
(Drawing by Andrea Salimbeti)

FORTIFICATIONS AND SIEGE WARFARE

One of the primary purposes of the prehistoric development of permanent sites of habitation was defence, as illustrated by the preponderance of settlements on naturally defensible terrain. The first major Aegean urban centres, complete with elaborate fortification systems, flourished in mainland Greece and the Cycladic islands by the second half of the 4th millennium BC.

The Early Bronze Age Aegean displays a large variation in community size and organization. Small villages (approximately 150–300 people) and scattered hamlets predominate, but in other regions large settlements with a considerable build-up of population (hundreds to the lower thousands) were present. The difference between large sites and average villages is indicated not only by size, but also by complexity of layout, differentiation in terms of scale and construction of some buildings, and by evidence of the centralization of some political, economical and military activities. Defensive warfare was already organized in a primitive fashion in the fortified settlements of the pre-Minoan cultures such as Kastraki and Dimini in Thessaly, Kastri and Panormos on the Cycladic islands of Syros and Naxos, and Lerna in Argolis.

The settlement that developed on Kastraki Hill and the area around it covered a large area of at least 100,000 sq. m during the Middle Neolithic Period. The stone foundations of blocks of houses are easily visible. The houses at Kastraki are usually small, with narrow passageways between them, in places forming squares. Outside Kastraki, in the settlement that extended to the west, the houses are rather more spacious with a clearly planned layout. This organized settlement comprised 500–800 houses. All houses have stone foundations, a clay brick superstructure, a pitched roof with beams covered by clay and a hole to emit smoke. The houses were surrounded by large walls, which should not, however, be thought of as defensive work, but merely as retaining walls.

In Dimini six curvilinear enclosures, not surviving in their entirety, indicate the phases of habitation development. They were built of local slate and were 0.6–1.4m wide. Their height was 1.5m where they were free standing, while at points where they functioned as house walls they reached 1.7m. They were arranged radially and were interrupted at four points by passages 0.85–1.1m wide, leading to the interior

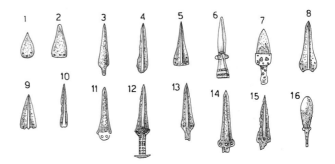

of the settlement. In this way activity could take place in five areas: the central courtyard and the four sections around it. The passages towards the central courtyard were slightly sloping and partially paved with slats.

During the most significant period, from 2700 to 2000 BC, the Aegean inhabitants lived in organized settlements and small citadels complete with a fortified wall and bulwark, towers and gates to provide protection against invaders from the sea or internal conflict between various settlements. Despite the absence of any sign of conflict or destruction, the small Cycladic forts presumably reflect the insecurity of the times. The architecture of those fortifications may be viewed as a miniaturized version of the great defensive circuits of earlier stages at sites such as Troy I–II, Limantepe and Lerna. One of the most remarkable fortified Cycladic citadels is Kastri on Syros. Located on a steep hilltop, its fortifications consist of a wall with six hollow projecting bastions built of small to medium slabs. Outside the wall there is a second defensive wall or breastwork. Entrance into the fort is gained through one of the bastions. The interior of the settlement consists of clusters of small rooms. Panormos on Naxos is another small fortification; the interior is irregular, with several roughly semicircular bastions and a single entrance from the east. There is no clear purpose to a pile of circular stones lying just outside this entrance. Mount Kynthos on Delosa was probably another small fort perched on a hill consisting of several bastions, within which were some irregularly shaped rooms and at least three small apsidal houses.

Selection of early Aegean daggers:
1) 5500 BC from Aya Marina
2) 4800 BC from Ayios Dimitrios
3) 4800–3300 BC from Dimini
4) 4800–3300 BC from Sesklo
5) 2800–2300 BC from Amorgos
6) 2000 BC from Cyprus
7) 2000–1800 BC from Kretes
8) 1700 BC from Haghia Triada
9) 2300–1900 BC from Mesara
10) 1700 BC from Psychro Cave
11) 1600 BC from Malia
12) 1700–1600 BC from Malia
13) 1700 BC from Haghios Onofrios
14) 1600 BC from Haghia Triada
15) 1600 BC from Haghia Triada
16) 1450–1400 BC from Archanes (razor).
(Drawing by Andrea Salimbeti)

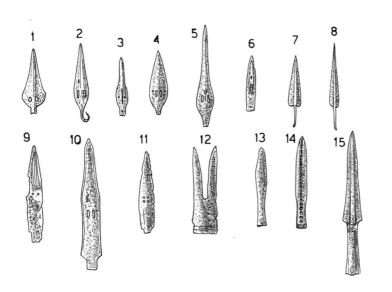

Selection of early Aegean spear points:
1) 2700–2300 BC from Amorgos
2) 2300 BC from Dokathismata
3) 2300 BC from Haghia Paraskevi
4) 2300–2000 BC from Amorgos
5) 2000 BC from Amorgos
6) 2000 BC from Sesklo
7) 2300–2000 BC from Vounous (Cyprus)
8) 1900–1700 BC from Vounous (Cyprus)
9) 2000–1800 BC from Malia
10) 1600 BC from Archanes
11) 1500 BC from Apolodou
12) 1500 BC from Haghios Onofrios
13) 1500 BC from Haghios Onofrios
14) 1500 BC from Archanes
15) 1500–1450 BC from Knossos.
(Drawing by Andrea Salimbeti)

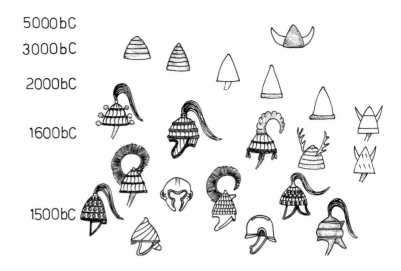

Selection of early Aegean helmets and caps from 5000 to 1500 BC, from frescos, finds and sculptures. (Drawing by Andrea Salimbeti)

5000 bC

3000 bC

2000 bC

1600 bC

1500 bC

Lerna is one of the largest (*c.*180 sq. m.) prehistoric mounds in southern Greece and probably owed its importance to its position on the narrow strip of land between sea and mountains that formed the route from the Argolid to the South Peloponnese. It is located in the marshy region on the Gulf of Argos (10km south of Argos). Early Bronze Age Lerna had substantial fortified walls and a palace or administrative centre in a central building referred to as the 'House of Tiles'. This was a large two-storey building with terracotta roof tiles and several storage rooms where clay sealings were found. In classical times the area was claimed as home of the Nereids, the place where Herakles slew the Hydra and the location of the entrance to Hades (through the Aleyonean Lake).

The major Cyprean settlements in the Bronze Age, located along the coast and in the central part of the island, were built as defensive fortresses, generally of square or rectangular design, surrounded by a massive wall about 6m high and closed on all four sides by defensive ramparts. All around the fortress were dwellings for the soldiers and the access gate was in some cases protected by a rectangular tower.

Archaeological surveys show that sites of habitation were more likely to be located away from the coast in the intermediate zone, suggesting Minoans felt vulnerable to attack from the sea, presumably by pirates. Further support comes from structures referred to as guardhouses or guard posts that are present both in the countryside and adjacent to settlements, and which appear to have had a defensive function. A different suggestion for the role of the guard posts and smaller sites, called *vigla* in modern times, was initially advanced by Arthur Evans – that they were established to exercise 'palatial control over the routes and therefore circulation' on Crete. In either case, they suggest some

Arrowheads from Phaistos, 16th century BC. Iraklion Archaeological Museum. (Author's photo, courtesy of the museum)

Type II variant B decorative dagger from Knossos, ex Evans 1921, dated by Evans to MM period (1700 BC), but most probably dated to LM IA or LM IB period (1500–1400 BC). The engraved bronze dagger blade shows a warrior engaged in a boar hunt and a fight between bulls. The handle attachment of many daggers was weak and many specimens, such as this, show breaks precisely at the points of the rivets holes.

degree of underlying social or political conflict. A differing view that is consistent with the peaceful Minoan model sees these structures as rest posts along communication routes, although some sites are located on largely inaccessible ridges. One example of a guard post lies on a ridge overlooking the Choiromandres Valley. It appears to belong to a 'network of isolated buildings of similar size and topography, whose aim was the control of the communication axes and the defense of the hinterland'. Another line of evidence is the presence of what are termed 'refuge sites' on almost inaccessible locations in regions that were accessible from the sea. These seem to have been secure places to which the inhabitants of local settlements could relocate in times of danger and insecurity.

Despite having found ruined watchtowers and fortification walls, Evans argued that there was little evidence for ancient Minoan fortifications. But, as S. Alexiou has pointed out, a number of sites, especially Early and Middle Minoan sites such as Haghia Photia, are built on hilltops or are otherwise fortified. According to Nowicki, quoting the example of Myrtos-Phyrgos, one of the hundreds of fortified sites already particularly common by the end of the Protopalatial Period, the history of the defensible and fortified sites in Crete is long and complex, and points to the tension between territories or states on the island as a whole, going back as far as the Prepalatial Period.

Clear evidence of the presence of fortifications in Neopalatial Crete is visible in the recently discovered clay seal of the Lord of Chanià (the 'Master Impression'), where a fortified structure, crowned with sacral horns, appears raised on the top of a cliff in front of the sea. Archaeological evidence of centres quickly fortified in emergency or against violent attack appears in particular from the end of MM II, with the construction of the defensive squared walls in Pyrgos where the area was furnished with two cisterns, and the discovery, in Malia, of metallic tripods hidden underground, as if the inhabitants feared a raid and tried to keep their most precious objects safe. Also, Walberg proposed a military cause for the second destruction of Phaistos Palace, linked with the classical Kamares MM II pottery.

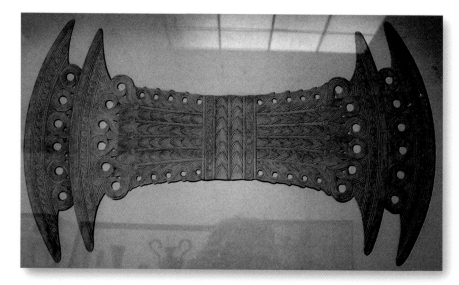

EARLY AEGEAN SHIPS AND THE NAVAL POWER OF CRETE

Early navigation in the Aegean has been testified by the tools made of Melian obsidian, which were found in Franchthi Cave in Hermionid (on the eastern coast of the Peloponnese), a distance of 80 nautical miles (approximately 150km) from Melos. Such tools, which have also been found on Crete (Knossos) and on Cyprus, substantiate the existence of sea routes in the Aegean from the Early to the Final Neolithic Period (6800–3200 BC).

A clay model from Palaikastro dated around 3000 BC is one of the earliest representations of an Aegean ship. In this model, one side of the hull terminates in a lofty vertical post, while the other, with no upright fixture at all, trails off into horizontal extension at the waterline. Another clay model from Mochlos dated around 3000–2700 BC represents a small craft with two stem-projecting forefoot together with raised stem. This kind of ship, distinguished by straight lines, angled ends and a lofty prow, seems to be the prototype for later Greek warships and merchant ships.

One of the earliest large Aegean ships is represented on some Cycladic terracotta 'frying pans' from Syros dated around 2500–2000 BC. This multi-oared galley has a long vertical prow with a fish symbol mounted on top, perhaps acting as a weather vane to detect wind direction. Also the cords or beams hanging below the fish symbol might conceivably act as some sort of wind catching device.

Large ships of similar design with fish symbols on top of their prow are very much in evidence in several Cycladic representations dated around 2500–2000 BC. A ship with a Cycladic-like design is also one of the symbols on the disc from Phaistos. On the Greek mainland a ship scene has been restored from three small pottery fragments from Iolkos dated in the Middle Helladic Period (about 2000–1700 BC). The polychrome design, according to the Cycladic tradition, shows a short vessel, thickly outlined, the reserved interior filled with a zigzag pattern; there is a stout curved ram on the prow and a steering oar.

A large number of Minoan seals dated around 2000–1500 BC show very different kinds of ships. Some of these ships also show an asymmetrical profile, a high stem at one end and low extension at the other. Even if, as a rule, the illustrations are very schematic, the repetition of certain details adds credibility to the depictions. For example the forked appearance of the lofty stem as well as the mast and the sail.

Several types of Aegean ship are depicted in the famous fresco from Akrotiri on Thera, dated around 1600 BC. One image shows a small boat with ten oars, one steering oar and a skipper or high-rank passenger. The sterns of the ships are long and slender with mysterious objects attached, similar to the Aegean 'frying pan ship'. If a storm blew up against the side of the vessel, the stem would catch the wind while the stern appendage dragged in the water, turning the vessel around until the stern pointed into the waves.

Another highly decorated medium-size ship shows the mast, the sail, two steering oars, some passengers and the 'ship's captain' in a cabin located at the back of the ship. The stern appendage was not present in the small and medium-size ships, but it seems to be a distinguishing feature of the large vessels. The captain, two attendants and some high-status passengers are usually represented wearing either tunics or long robes. The representations of the large ship also show the stern appendage, long stem with ornaments, central feature and captain's cabin. On top of the cabin's central pole a strange object that seems to be a boar's tusk helmet is placed. In the ships from Thera, these cabins were placed at the back of the ship; for this reason these features have been also identified as cabins for 'VIPs' or items of ceremonial significance. It is even possible to interpret them as emblems of the religious leader of the largest ship.

Based on the artistic representations discovered to date, the Minoan fleet thus appears to have been mainly a trading fleet, but with weapons for defence against pirates.

Seal found in Padiasos, Crete, dated around 1460 BC. This is an early representation of a dual-chariot in Crete, where it was probably introduced by the Achaeans. This chariot was one of the most widely used in the Aegean region. It is characterized by semicircular extensions attached to the back of the chariot box. These extensions were unknown outside Greek-influenced regions. They were probably made from heat-bent wood with either fabric or oxhide stretched across the frame. The box also seems to have had the same covering, which enclosed it on three sides. Iraklion Archaeological Museum. (Author's photo, courtesy of the museum)

THE LIFE OF A WARRIOR

Duties in the palaces and abroad

So far only controversial evidence exists for a possible Minoan army, and no evidence at all for Minoan domination of peoples outside Crete. Having accepted, however, the idea of an elite warrior class, its conventions would not be very different from those existing during the same period in Asia Minor and the Fertile Crescent.

War was conceived not only as a necessity, but also as a duty. Crete, a maritime power, would have defended itself against pirates and commercial competitors, and also extended its markets and business through violence. Wars were conducted to obtain slaves for manpower.

On the island every city and palace fighting for hegemony would have had to suppress internal riots and keep its borders with its neighbours under control. Even if we accept that the Neopalatial Period in Crete was an age of

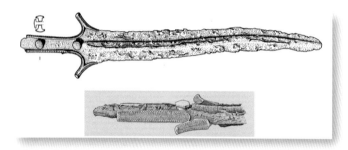

Ci-type sword from Phaistos Crete, Tombe dei Nobili, dated about 1450 BC, ex Savignon. This sword is 43cm long and its hilt and horns are decorated with an engraved gold lamina. Gold is still present on one of the bronze rivets of the handgrip; the sword probably belonged to a man, one of the dominant new Achaean elite in Crete. (Author's collection)

relative peace, the duties of the warrior elite were directed towards surveillance of the watchtowers and to maintaining the palace status quo.

Various archaeological findings and classical sources confirm the existence of rural communities organized in clans, obliged to support and maintain the three main dominant classes: a) the king, his family and courtiers; b) the clergy, both priestess and priests, and c) the military, formed by defence troops, naval infantry, instructors and officers.

Leisure activities

Sport and hunting were the favourite leisure activities of Aegean warriors. One of the most practised sports in Crete and a central attraction of Aegean society was bull leaping, very often represented in Minoan art. This ritual sport was conducted by young athletes – boys and girls – with the sacral bull and consisted of dangerous acrobatic leaps over the animal. These rituals were a sacral pastime in which warriors were probably also trained to prove their bravery.

A conical rhyton found in the royal palace of Haghia Triada is decorated with a scene depicting boxers. Some of them are heavily equipped, with gloves and low-profile 'hollow-eyed' helmets, as well as banded boots. Some others – who are depicted with slimmer bodies – have only small plumed caps for head protection. A third category of young fighters has no protection on head and hands. Maybe the Minoans were the first to have different categories of boxing? Anyway these games, as well as the bull leaping, certainly had a solemn religious significance. Boxing is often represented in Minoan art as a display of physical strength, ability and a symbol of victory. These competitions were passed on from the Minoans to the Achaeans, and were also mentioned by Homer in the *Iliad* as funeral games in honour of Patroclus.

Hunting, the bow exercise and running resulted in the young Minoans developing the slim, brawny and muscular bodies represented in their art. Hunting was the most common sport, true training for war; capturing

G **LATE MINOAN WARRIOR, 1700–1450 BC**
(1) This heavily armoured Gortyna warrior is based on a statuette from Khanià, found in a rural villa near Gortyna. His military accoutrement shows the strong influence of the mainland Achaeans. He is wearing a bronze cuirass, spear and elaborate helmet reconstructed from the Katsamba vase. The armour is an early type of bell-shaped cuirass, worn over a garment with fringed edges. It shows similarities with the breast plate of the Dendra armour from Argolis, and a stone vessel in the shape of a cuirass from the 'Tomb of the gold and silver cup' at Knossos. His precious sword is slung across the breast through a baldric. His figure-of-eight body shield is based on pottery representations and reconstructed according to fragments from the Cretan warrior graves of Aghios Nikolaos. (2) The Haghia Triada palace guard is based on one of the figures engraved in the Haghia Triada cup. This warrior is equipped with a long A-type sword. In his left hand he is carrying a sort of plumed stick, probably a command insignia. He is also wearing a gold torque around the neck, probably a symbol of rank, and high boots.

In the background some examples of swords (Malia, Aghioi Teodoroi, Ialysos), daggers (Aghios Onophrios, Haghia Triada, Haghia Triada), spear points (Archanes, Knossos, Aghios Onophrios) and helmets (Haghia Triada, Phaistos, Zakros) are also illustrated. The reconstruction of a proto-Dipylon shield is based on the gold ring of the 'treasure of Aigina' and pendants from Crete.

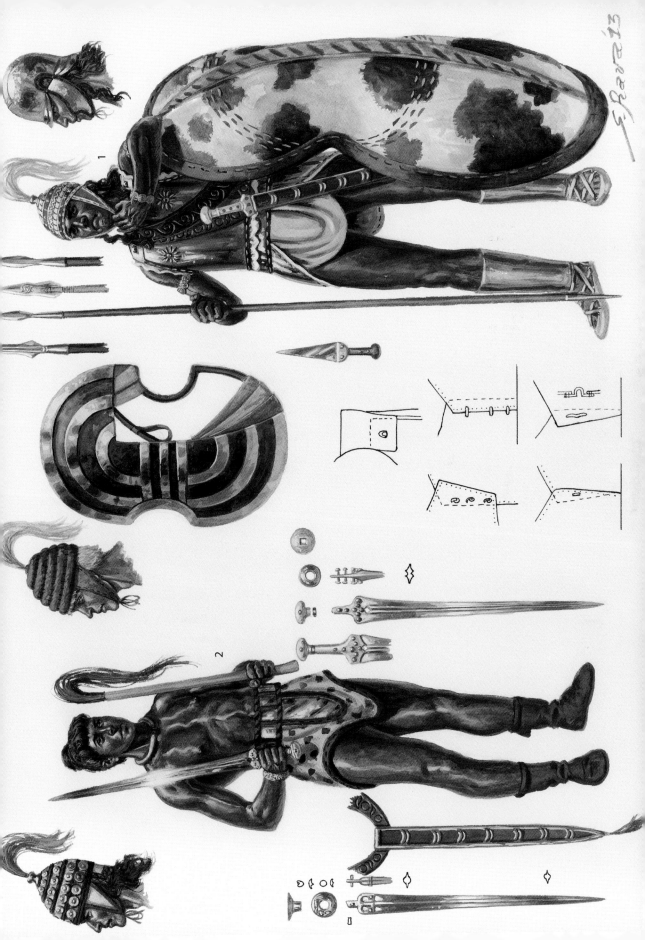

Fresco of the 'black guard' from Knossos, dated 1450 BC. Iraklion Archaeological Museum. (Author's photo, courtesy of the museum)

wild bulls – as on the gold Vaphiò Cup – was one of the most fascinating. Hunting birds was probably also widely practised.

The very high level of freedom enjoyed by Minoan women of the age allowed them to attend games and sports.

Training and discipline

Signs of warfare appear in Minoan art and armed warriors are depicted being stabbed in the throat with swords, with violence possibly also occurring in the context of ritual or blood sport. The initiation retirement and the individual deed were probably characteristics of the warrior class in Crete, as can be suggested by various elements, such as the weapons deposits in caves (Arkalochori, Psychro, Ida), the myth of Theseus (coming from Athens to Crete for his war initiation together with 14 other young boys) or the rituals surviving in the classical age (such as the Athenian *Oschophoriai*, held in honour of Ariadne and Dyonisos). At Phaistos, still in the classical age, a festival of probable Minoan origin was held. It was called the *Ekdisiai*. During this festival young boys discard their childhood garments; this tradition was linked to the local cult of the pre-Hellenic Goddess Leto-Pitia.

Hunting was the usual training for warriors, as confirmed by artistic representation and mythological tradition (Androgeus, son of Minos, taming the wild bull). Sometimes young warriors were trained to hunt in extreme and difficult conditions. To survive they had to use their skill, such as employing tricks and booby traps. The main purpose of these practices was to create elite skilled and strong fighters, good hunters, bowmen and experts in weapons and martial art.

A possible depiction of early martial arts seems to be featured on a Cycladic figurine from the Cycladic II Period (about 2800–2300 BC), which shows a warrior drawing a dagger with his left hand and blocking with his right. The seals and the iconography of weapons in art are very informative about the identification of warrior types and technology; it is possible to distinguish archers (distance fighting), spear fighters (medium-distance combat), sword fighters (close combat) and sword fighters with spears (combined medium-distance and close combat), in order to get an impression of the different specialities comprising a warrior's training.

Analysis of sword types could interestingly reveal details of types of combat and related training. With type A, the weight is far forward of the handle; if the sword was held horizontally during the fight, this would put a lot of pressure on the handle rivets and also on the wrist and elbow joints of the user. A heavy, front-weighted blade creates a lot of inertia, which inevitably lengthens all the movements. This, according to Peatfield, suggests that the two main ways the A-type swords could be used were: a) long-range cutting and thrusting, and

b) wide/circular open-arc slashes. These are slow movements and are best suited to single-combat duelling. Sometimes this has suggested the idea that the A-type swords were not functional at all, but rather used only as ritual implements or symbols. In a room in Malia (protopalatial sale β), interpreted as a sacrifice or libation shrine, two examples of these swords have been found. Although the use of swords for sacrifice in Minoan Crete is very much in evidence, the sacralization of swords does not exclude their martial use.

The development of the full tang in B-type swords not only strengthened the handle, rendering the sword able to survive the clash of sword-on-sword or sword-on-armour contact, but it also radically altered the weapon's balance, by shifting more of the weight towards the hand. This was the reason for the disproportionate widening of the blade at the guard. The closer the point of balance falls to the handle, the easier and faster a sword can be deployed, causing less stress on the wrist and elbow and increasing the variety of strokes a swordsman can make.

The longer C-type was probably similar in use to the long-range, cut-and-thrust of type A. In this sense the horned guards were particularly useful. To avoid problems, such as bending the blade under prolonged sword-on-sword clashes or frontal impact on armour or bone, a fighting style was developed that avoided clashing with the opponent's sword, but parried and deflected it. Thus opposed blades tended to slide along one another and aggressive cuts were made through forward strokes, especially to the limbs. It is surely no coincidence that the study of Minoan warrior graves has revealed evidence of injuries to the weapon-wielding arm.

Fragment of marble rhyton from Epidauros found together with EH–LH ceramics and idols. At lower right a ship's cabin is represented. At the base of square, a dolphin prow rears up. To the left is the shoreline where men are depicted marching. At the lower left there are at least two men behind body shields with long batons or spears. (Drawing by Andrea Salimbeti ex Wedde)

Minoan clay sealing from Kydonia from the 15th century BC, representing a minotaur armed with a mace or club. Khanià Archaeological Museum. (Author's photo, courtesy of the museum)

Belief and belonging

Most of our knowledge of Aegean prehistoric religion is based on highly questionable hypotheses, the archaeological evidence being scarce and correct interpretation of the material very difficult. However general characteristics of Aegean religion may be understood through analogy with the Near East. Both these societies developed from similar Neolithic farming cultures and many of their basic activities and mentality would have remained the same, reflecting similarities in their religious beliefs. Thus they believed in supernatural powers that could control the weather, the productivity of the soil and the fertility of living creatures. Gifts, offerings of food, drink and living creatures were given or promised to the gods during public ceremonies as well as household rituals and 'magical' practices.

In some communities, such as the Lerna III settlement, a loosely organized 'animistic' form of religion, largely based on the home, may have developed. There are in fact a number of open-air sites where this could have been practised, apart from those associated with tombs. There is very little evidence of religious practice in the Cyclades and on the Greek mainland before the Minoan Second Palace Period.

The Minoan belief system was extremely complex. It evolved out of the Neolithic

THE ACHAEAN CONQUEST OF KNOSSOS, 1430 BC

(1) The Minoan prince, whose costume and headgear is copied from the famous Prince of Lilies, is equipped with a hypothetical reconstruction of a linen corselet reinforced with bronze plates, as found in Arkalochori. He is dressed with the typical loin covering of the Minoans, a tight metal belt that seems to be padded inside, and a double apron that reaches halfway down the thigh at the back, merely covering the leather sheath present underneath in the front. Note his elaborate headdress, made from a row of lilies with innumerable stamens projecting. The flower is considered to be a combination of the lily with the Egyptian flowering rush called the papyrus. Another lily projects from the crown, from which, in turn, three long peacock feathers emerge. He is bearing a small rectangular shield based on a seal from Knossos and a typical Minoan double axe.

(2) The Achaean warlord is equipped with copper or bronze banded armour tentatively reconstructed using the fragmented plates from Phaistos (Tombe dei Nobili) and the Achaean cuirass represented in the Linear B tablets from Knossos. The corselet has overlapping bands, running lengthwise, and in the lower part a larger abdomen protector (*zosteres*). These elements are sewn upon a linen or leather background with linen laces.

He is also equipped with a padded helmet and a full figure-of-eight body shield. The padded conical helmet with neck protection, large throat strap and horsetail is from a marble fragment from the island of *Keos*. **(3)** The Achaean charioteer is driving a dual-chariot as represented in the seal from Pediasos.

Statuette representing an armoured warrior, found in a Minoan rural villa in Khanià near Gortyna and dated to the second half of the 15th century BC. The date is prior to the destruction of the Cretan palaces and shows the influence of the Knossian Achaeans. (Ex Doro Levi, courtesy of ICEVO library)

Cretan religion. The evidence of sites of ritual activity can be divided into four broad categories: buildings that are or incorporate shrines, open-air sites (mainly peak sanctuaries), caves and tombs; all of these categories are well attested to in Crete. The commonest ritual actions seem to be the offering of clay objects. Other rites may have taken place as part of major ceremonies including libations, animal sacrifice and in some cases possibly even human sacrifice. Several cult objects are associated with the Minoan religion, such as clay votive bells or horned masks, wheel-made bovid figurines, bronze or gold double axes, horns of consecration, sacral knots and pillars.

The importance of public ceremonies would surely guarantee special status to those who acted as intermediaries between the community and supernatural powers. One of the major developments in Minoan religion is the emergence of a priestly class, clearly identifiable in artistic representations by dress and other details of appearance or activities. Its origin is probably identifiable from the Prepalatial Period from persons with whom figurines and other ritual items were buried, and whose tombs may have been cult centres. The representations and other evidence show that it included both men and women, and both sexes probably played a dominant role in some rituals. This is a notable contrast with the great Near Eastern religions, in which (although women could hold important positions) priests were generally male.

Weapons can have different functions and meaning, other than being the means of killing and defence: they can be objects of value through their artistic quality or symbols of power, prestige and authority, of sacrifice, reward or religious meaning. Thus the depositing of sheet swords in the Arkalochori Cave, together with the dozen or so golden double axes and the many silver and bronze examples found with them, can be explained as ritual practice. Daggers had symbolic meaning too. Their association with the dead in the grave suggests that even in death the ownership of a dagger contributes to social identity.

The context in which the weapons are found and the way of depositing them can often give a clue to their meaning, offering insight into the structure of early Aegean society. Shields and helmets, depicted in certain contexts, were, for example, religious symbols. Deities are sometimes shown with sword, spear or shield; sometimes the objects appear alone, as if standing in for an absent deity. Large figure-of-eight shields were depicted on the walls of the East Wing of the Labyrinth, possibly indicating that the building was under divine protection. Some ritual vessels have shields painted on them.

During the Second Palace Period the complex iconography detected in the depictions and the elaboration of the rituals indicate the sophistication that the Minoan religion had achieved by this time. During this period several representations of deities or impersonators of gods, such as the so-called 'Lady of Myrtos', 'Mountain Mother', 'Priest King' and 'Master Impression', are attested to on clay vessels, frescoes, seal-rings or seal-stones.

The main goddess of the Minoan pantheon is named Potnia, also called the 'Lady of the Labyrinth' in Knossos. She had shrines or sanctuaries in many places and was worshipped at least in the later part of the Minoan Period. The double axe was probably Potnia's symbol, and possibly the pillar and the snake were her symbols too. In her identity as a domestic goddess and guardian of households and cities, Potnia lived on as Athena, Rhea and Hera.

WARFARE

In the Palaeolithic Age weapons were mainly used for hunting, but also during clashes between different tribal groups.

The beginning of the Neolithic Age saw the invention of powerful weapons that would remain in use for the following centuries: the bow, sling, spear, mace and axe. Evidence of early fighting is seen in human remains showing the lethal effects of maces and similar weapons in such conflicts. Middle Bronze Age Lerna material is instructive in this respect: here Angel noted injuries on ten per cent of all skeletal material and another ten per cent of adults had evidence of thrusting wounds.

In the very Early Bronze Age Aegean settlements a uniform set of weapons was not commonly found in graves and depictions of professional warriors and scenes of combat are conspicuously absent. Most of the early Aegean communities could have recruited only small fighting forces for local conflicts, such as competing for resources, grievances between individuals, revenge or trespassing on territory (even if these disputes were not part of a general expansion strategy). In the course of pre-war activities, war parties were more likely to have been recruited with persuasion rather than force.

Warriors in tribal societies engaged in war with a combination of objectives, including, most frequently, trophies, booty or women. In any case, individual reasons motivated them. War parties were small – probably five to ten men in the case of villages and up to 50 for major settlements – and had short-term and simple one-tier leadership. Participants prepared their weapons and supplies themselves. All warriors took part in pre-war rituals and public feasting. Offensive tactics included assaults on individual enemy settlements, which were sometimes some distance away. Fighting with long- and middle-range weapons without direct contact predominated – hit-and-run raids and ambushes were preferred. Different types of weaponry, such as bows, slings and javelins, were normally used during these offensives.

In very early Minoan Crete the military leaders had small groups of foot-warriors, sling-men and bowmen under their command, as well as spearmen and warriors armed with short swords. These war parties practised raiding warfare, consisting of rapid action, raids and ambushes. War campaigns were mostly conducted during the fine seasons. Conquered settlements were sacked and completely destroyed by fire. When skeletons are not found on site, archaeologists assume that the inhabitants were taken into slavery and deported. The system of total destruction of the settlement excludes any possibility of ransom. The conquered lands and their farmers were divided between the palace leaders, priests and warriors to whom the king granted property.

The weapons can supply us with information about the nature of warfare and changes in the methods of conflict. For instance, swords used for cutting and slashing suggest fighting on foot, also confirmed by the early Minoan seals showing combat scenes. The combination of spear, for initial clash, sword for closer contact and dagger as a weapon of last resort, together with a shield, seem to have been standard equipment in the Minoan world.

Moreover, having warriors armed with thrusting spears, we can also tentatively infer group tactics, such as combat in close formation and coordinated action, as suggested by the marching warriors of the Akrotiri fresco. This fresco seems to suggest that – unlike the usual tactics from the

East, mainly consisting of throwing missiles, followed by close combat with no proper strong battle array – the Minoans had already discovered the secret of cohesive battle formations (possibly a proto-phalanx). The fresco of Thera suggests the employment of a dense battle scheme, formed by a compact array of men – armed with very long spears behind their shields – against the more chaotic attack of their enemy from the sea (possibly Lybians). The only prototype of a similar tactic can be seen on the Sumerian 'Vulture Stele' of Lagash dated about 2500 BC. By comparison with the Sumerian tactical model we can assume this proto-phalanx was composed of companies of 36 to 100 men.

In any case, this iconographic source, together with the fresco of the Captain of the Blacks from Knossos, illustrates that Late Bronze Aegeans at least appreciated the military advantages of the column.

The structure of some early Aegean fortifications implies open, all-out attacks along the front of the defence wall. Elaborate and massive structures like bastions (providing firing positions to protect the base of the wall and weak points at the entrances) or stone facing on the lower slopes of the settlements as a base for a mud-brick fortification wall on a higher level should be noted. The fortification of Troy II is a classical example, but similar fortification strategies seem to have also been used at other eastern Aegean sites. Consequently, the tactics of massed and concentrated assaults were feared enough to bring about new strategies for defence. Large bastions served probably also as barracks, storage facilities and administrative buildings and could be regarded as symbols of incipient military institution.

Post-war activities concentrate on ritual observances for people who killed in battle, such as isolation, cleansing or abstinence. Only after those observances do the successful warriors receive higher status. Victory feasts follow purification. All of the dead were retrieved, but there is no sign of the treatment of the bodies of those killed in warfare being any different from any others.

Warfare also needs to be connected with seafaring activities. Longboats and large canoes have been recognized as high-status sea craft employed in warfare, raiding and possibly prestigious travel. We can thus postulate that individuals of warrior status would also have been involved in seafaring, an activity additionally associated with the movement of goods and the control of maritime traffic.

Longboat activity played a part in the prosperity and survival of Cycladic communities, while at the same time they provided the social arena in which seafarers/warriors could have achieved their status through glorification. The association of the representation of longboats and exceptionally rich graves also indicates the role of seafaring in the attainment of high social status.

SITES, MUSEUMS AND ELECTRONIC RESOURCES

Athens – the National Archaeological Museum.
Crete – Iraklion hosts the main archaeological museum, with an astonishing amount of Minoan material. Many military objects and images of warriors and weaponry can be seen in the Archaeological Museum of Chanià and the Malia Archaeological Museum; the sites of Knossos, Phaistos and Haghia Triada are a must-see.
Cyprus – there are four archaeological museums where relevant cultural material is well illustrated.
London – the British Museum.
The main web resource for weaponry of the Bronze Age in Greece can be found on the authors' website www.salimbeti.com/micenei/index.htm, where you can also find the most relevant links to other websites related to this subject, along with a complete bibliography.

BIBLIOGRAPHY

Andreadaki-Vlazaki, M., *The county of Khania, through its monuments*, Athens (2000)

Andreadaki-Vlazaki, M. & Protopapadaki, E., Kouklaki Excavation, *73–77 Igoumenou Gabriel Street, Khanià, Khanià (Kydonia), a Tour of sites of ancient memories, 16*, Khanià (2010)

Borchardt, J., *Homerische Helme*, Mainz (1972)

Cawkwell, G., *Thucydides and the Peloponnesian War*, New York (1997)

Cassola, P. G., *Le armi defensive dei Micenei nelle figurazioni*, Roma (1973)

Cassola, P. G., *Nuovi Studi sulle armi dei Micenei*, Roma (1992)

Connolly, P., *The Greek Armies*, Oxford (1977)

Constantakopoulou, C., *The dance of the islands, insularity, networks, the Athenian Empire and the Aegean world*, Oxford (2007)

D'Agata, A. L., 'Hidden wars: Minoans and Myceneans at Haghia Triada in the LM III period: the evidence from pottery' in Polemos, *le contexte guerrier en égée à l'âge du bronze, Actes de la 7e rencontre égéenne internationale Université de Liège, 14–17 avril 1998*, Liège (1999), pp. 47–55

D'Amato R. & Salimbeti A., *Bronze Age Greek Warrior, 1600–1100 B.C.*, Oxford (2011)

Demargne, P., *Arte Egea*, Milano (1964)

Dickinson, O. 'Robert Drew's theories about the nature of warfare in the late Bronze Age' in Polemos, *le contexte guerrier en égée à l'âge du bronze, Actes de la 7e rencontre égéenne internationale Université de Liège, 14–17 avril 1998*, Liège (1999), pp. 21–29

Dörpfeld, W. & Goessler, P., *Alt-Ithaka: ein Beitrag zur Homer-Frage; Studien und Ausgrabungen auf der Insel Leukas-Ithaka, II Bände*, München-Gräfelfing (1927)

Driessen, J. & Macdonald, C. F., 'Some Military Aspects of the Aegean in the Late Fifteenth and Early Fourteenth Centuries B.C.' in BSA 79 (1984), pp. 49–74

Driessen, J., 'The Archaeology of the Aegean Warfare' in Polemos, *le contexte guerrier en égée à l'âge du bronze, Actes de la 7e rencontre égéenne internationale Université de Liège, 14–17 avril 1998*, Liège (1999), pp. 11–20

Evans, A., *The Palace of Minos: a comparative account of the successive stages of the early Cretan civilization as illustrated by the discoveries at Knossos. Volume I: The Neolithic and Early and Middle Minoan Ages*, London (1921)

Evans, A., *The Palace of Minos: a comparative account of the successive stages of the early Cretan civilization as illustrated by the discoveries at Knossos. Volume II: Fresh lights on origin and external relations*, London (1928)

Evans, A., *The Palace of Minos: a comparative account of the successive stages of the early Cretan civilization as illustrated by the discoveries at Knossos. Volume III: The great transitional age in the northern and eastern sections of the Palace*, London (1930)

Evans, A., *The Palace of Minos: a comparative account of the successive stages of the early Cretan civilization as illustrated by the discoveries at Knossos. Volume IV Part II: Camp-stool fresco, long-robed priests and beneficent genii, Chryselephantine Boy-God and ritual hair-offering; Intaglio Types, M.M. III–L. M. II, late hoards of sealings, deposits of inscribed tablets and the palace store; Linear Script B and its mainland extension, Closing Palatial Phase; Room of Throne and final catastrophe*, London (1935)

Faure, P., *La vita quotidiana a Creta ai tempi di Minosse (1500 a.C.)*, Milano (1991)

Finkelberg, M., 'Greek epic tradition on population movements in Bronze Age Greece' in Polemos, *le contexte guerrier en égée à l'âge du bronze, Actes de la 7e rencontre égéenne internationale Université de Liège, 14–17 avril 1998*, Liège (1999), pp. 31–37

Godart, L., 'La fin des premiers Palais Crétois: lutte intestine ou tremblement de terre' in Polemos, *le contexte guerrier en égée à l'âge du bronze, Actes de la 7e rencontre égéenne internationale Université de Liège, 14–17 avril 1998*, Liège (1999), pp. 39–45

Grguric, N., *The Myceneans, c.1650–1100 BC*, Oxford (2005)

Hiller, S., 'Pax Minoica versus Minoan Thalassocracy: Military Aspects of Minoan Culture' in Haegg, R. & Marinatos, N. (eds.), *The Minoan Thalassocracy: Myth and Reality. Proceedings of the Third International Symposium at the Swedish Institute in Athens, 31 May – 5 June 1982*, Skrifter utgivna av Svenska Institutet i Athen 4, 32, Goeteborg (1983), pp. 27–31

Höckmann, O., '*Lanze und Speer* im Spätminoischen und Mykenischen Griechenland' in *JbRGZM* 27 (1980), pp. 13–158

Hood, S. 'Shaft Grave Swords: Mycenaean or Minoan?' in *Pepragmena tou D' Diethnous Kretologikou Synedriou*, Athens (1980), I, pp. 234–237

Houston, M. G., *Ancient Greek, Roman and Byzantine costume & decoration*, London (1977)

Karageorghis, V., *Cipro*, Milano (2002)

Karykas, P., *Ancient military technique (6000–146 a.C)*, n. 32, Polemikes Monografies, Athens (2003) (in Greek)

Kilian-Dirlmeier, I., *Die Schwerter in Griechenland (außerhalb der Peloponnes), Bulgarien und Albanen*, Stuttgart (1993)

Levi, D., 'La villa rurale minoica di Gortina' in *Bollettino d' arte*, 1959, n.3, pp. 237–265

Liritzis, Y. & Galloway, R. B., 'Thermoluminescence dating of Neolithic Sesklo and Dimini, Thessaly, Greece' in *P.A.C.T Journal* (1982) 6, pp. 450–459

Liritzis, Y. & Dixon, J., 'Cultural contacts between Neolithic settlements of Sesklo and Dimini, Thessaly' in *Anthropologika* (1984) 5, pp. 51–62 (in Greek)

Marinatos, N., *Art and Religion in Thera, reconstructing a bronze age society*, Athens (1984)

Martin J. & Denoel, J., *Le costume antique (1)*, Pantin (1999)

Mina, M., 'In search of the Cycladic hunter-warrior: evidence and implications for the understanding of gender construction and roles in the Early Bronze Age Aegean' in Dommasnes, L.H., Hjørungdal, T., Montón-Subías, S., Sánchez Romero, M. & Wicker, N. L. (eds.), *Situating Gender in European Archaeologies (Archaeolingua, Series Minor)*, Budapest (2010), pp. 225–244

Molloy, B., 'Martial arts and materiality: a combat archaeology perspective on Aegean swords of the fifteenth and fourteenth centuries BC' in *World Archaeology* 40(1): pp. 116–134

Panstwowy Institut Wydawniczy, *Kultura wysp Cykladzkich w epoce brazu*, Warszawa (1986)

Peatfield, A., 'The Paradox of violence: weaponry and martial art in Minoan Crete' in Polemos, *le contexte guerrier en égée à l'âge du bronze, Actes de la 7e rencontre égéenne internationale Université de Liège, 14–17 avril 1998*, Liège (1999), pp. 67–75

Popham, M. R., Catling, E.& Catling, H. W., 'Sellopoulo tombs 3 and 4, two late Minoan graves near Knossos' in *BSA* 69 (1974), pp. 195–258

Sandars, N. K., 'The First Aegean Swords and Their Ancestry' in *American Journal of Archaeology* Vol 65 No. 1 (January 1961), pp. 17–29

Savignoni, L., 'Scavi e scoperte nella necropoli di Phaestos' in *Monumenti Anichi della Reale Accademia dei Lincei*, XIV, Milano (1905), col. 501–666

Snodgrass, A., *Arms and Armour of the Greeks*, Ithaca-NY (1967)

Soles, J. F., 'The collapse of Minoan civilization: the evidence of the broken Ashlar' in Polemos, *le contexte guerrier en égée à l'âge du bronze, Actes de la 7e rencontre égéenne internationale Université de Liège, 14–17 avril 1998*, Liège (1999), pp. 57–64

Thanasis Papdopoulos, J., *The Late Bronze Age Daggers of the Aegean, I – The Greek Mainland*, Stuttgart (1998)

Wiener, M., 'The tale of the conical cups' in Hagg, R. and Marinatos, N. *Crete and the Cyclads in LM1, Myth and reality* (1984), pp. 17–26

INDEX

References to illustrations and plates are shown in **bold**. Captions to plates are shown in brackets.

Achaeans 5, 8, 10, 14, 19, 29; and armour 39, 41, 43–44; invasion of **57** (56)
Aegean Sea 7, 10, 12, 15, 16, 23–24, 45 (44), 50
Aegina 41, 43
Akrotiri fresco 27–28, **30**, **31**, **33** (32), 39, 41, 51, 59–60
Amorgos 26, 32, 38
Anatolia 5, 7, 23, 36, 28, 40
animal skins 20, 22, 39, 42; see also leather
archaeology 4, 10, 12, 48, 49
Archanes 27
archers **26**, 41, 43
Argolis 31, 44, 46
Arkalochori Cave 36, 43, 54, 58
armour **53** (52), **57** (56), 58; body 42–44; helmets **21** (20), **25** (24), **31**, **33** (32), 35, 40–42, **44**, 48; shields **9** (8), **29**, 38–40, **42**, **43**, **44**
Asia Minor 4, 6, 7, 12, 51
Ayios Ioannis 19, 39

Balkans, the 24, 38
belts 20, 22, 32
blades 26–27, 28, 30, 34, 36
boar's tusks 35, 40–41, 42, 43
body paint 20, **21** (20); see also tattoos
bronze 4, 16, 23, 27, 28, 29, 38, 39, 42
Bronze Age 4, 6–7, 14, 24, 26, 28, 29, 34, 35, 59
bull leaping 52
burial rites 6, 14, 38

'Captain of Blacks' fresco **14**, **54**, 60
Chalcolithic Era 6
chariots 14, **25** (24), 51
clay 4, 35, 41, 46, 48, 50, 58
clothing **9** (8), **17** (16), 20, 22, **57** (56); and women **33** (32); see also armour: body; loincloths
copper 4, 5, 6, 7, **14**, 15, 16, 23, 28, 29, 36, 44
Crete 5, 7–8, 10, 14, 18, 50, 52; and armour 40, 41, 42; and clothing 20, 22; and fortified settlements 48–9; and military organization 19, 51–2, 54; and religion 58; and warriors **33** (32); and weaponry 26–27, 28, 29, 30–32, 34, 36, 37, 38; see also Minoans
Cyclades, the 4–5, 15, 16, 40, 50, 60; and military organization 12–13, **14**, **16**, 22, 54; settlements **17** (16), 46, 47; and weaponry 30, 32, 36, 38
Cyprus 5–7, 26, 28, 36, 48, 50

defence 46, 47, 48, 60
deities 28, 58
Diktaian Cave 36
Dimini 4, 5, 23, 26, 32, 46, 47

Egypt 4, 7, 14
Epirus 39
Evans, Sir Arthur 8, 15, 31, 48, 49

farming 4, 5, 6, 12, 56
festivals 54, 60
fortified settlements 6–7, 12, 46, 47, 48–49, 60
Franchthi Cave 50
frescoes 38, 54; see also Akrotiri fresco

genealogy 10
graves 12, 13, 14, 19, 26, 36, 38, 41, 43, 55, 58
guardhouses 48–49

Haghia Photia 49
Haghia Triada 28, 29, 31, 34, 35, 36, 37, 39, 41, 42, 43, **44**, 52
hair 21 (20)
headgear **12**, 22; see also armour: helmets
Heraklion 41
Herodotus 15
hieroglyphics 37
Hisarlik Hill 36, 40
Homer 52
horses 12, 14
housing 4, 46–47
hunter-warriors 12–13, **14**, **16**, 20, 22, 37
hunting 5, 24, 52, 54, 59

Indo-Europeans 8, **25** (24)
Ionian islands 4, 30
ivory 34, 41, 42

jewellery **21** (20), 22, 42

Kastraki Hill 46
Kastri-Chalandriani **17** (16), 46, 47
Ke-re-te 8, 10, 14, **21** (20)
Kea 12, 41
Kephala 42
Keros-Syros culture 36
Khanià-Kydonia 19, 22, 38, **40**, 44
Khirokitia culture 5
Knossos 8, 14, 18, 19, 27, 28, 37, 38, 39, 41, 42, 43, **54**, 58, 60; conquest of **57** (56)

'Lady of the Labyrinth' 58
leather 20, 38, 39, 40, 42
Lerna 46, 47, 48, 56, 59
linen 20, 38, 40, 42, 44
loincloths 20, **21** (20), 22
Lord of Chanià 49
Loutraki 36
Lybians **33** (32)

mainland Greece 4, 7, 10, 18–19, 46; and armour 42; and migration **25** (24); and military organization 12; and seafaring 50; and weaponry 26–27, 36
Malia 30, 34, 37, 49
maritime trade 6, 15, 16
Mediterranean Sea 7, 15, 16
Melos 4, 50
Mesopotamia 4, 7
Messara 34
metallurgy 6, 7, 12–13, 23–24
migration 4, 6, 8, 10, **25** (24)
military organization 12–14, 19, 59
Minoans 5, 7–8, 18–19, 20, 41, 52; and fortified settlements 48–9; and military organization 14, 51, **53** (52), 54, 59–60; and religion 10, 56, 58; and seafaring 50–51; and thalassocracy 15–16, **45** (44); and weaponry 26–27, 28, 29, 30–32, 34–35, 36, 37, 38
Minos, King 8, 15, 16
Mochlos 10, 36, 50
mosaics **26**, 37
Mount Kynthos 47
Mycenae 30

Naxos 12, 23, 29, 32, 46, 47
Near East 6, 23, 56, 58
Neolithic Period 35, 37, 38, 40, 46, 50, 59; settlements 4, 5, 6, 20, 23–24
New Hospital 19, 39

obsidian 4, 6, 35, 37–38, 50

Palaikastro 50
Palatial Periods 29, 36, 42, 49, 51–52, 58
Paleolithic Period 23, 59
Panormos 46, 47
Peloponnese 10, 48, 50
Phaistos 28, 31, 36, 38, 41, 44, 49, 54; Disc 36, 37, 40, 50
Philia culture 36
Phocis 23
piracy 15, 16, **45** (44), 48, 51
Polycrates of Samos 15
population figures 12, 19, 46
Potnia 58
pottery 4, 5, 15 **29**, 36, 39, **40**, 49, 50; see also vases
prestige goods 12, 13
Proto-Hellenes 8, 10
Pyrgos 49

religion 6, 7, 10, 19, 29, 36, 52, 56, 58
Rhodes 27, 31
rhyton **32**, 41, 52, 55
rituals 54, 58, 59, 60

Sanatorium 38
seafaring 4, 16, 28, 50–51, 60
seals 6, 22, 27, 28, 37, 39, 40, 42, 43, **44**, 49
Sesklo 4, **9** (8), 12, 23, 26, 32, 35, 40
settlements 12, 59; see also fortified settlements
ships **45** (44), 50–51, 55
Sicily 15
Sotira culture 5
statuettes 6, **12**, 14, **16**, 32, **58**
stone 28, 36
symbolism 12, 50
Syro-Palestine 5, 7
Syros 12, **17** (16), 46, 47, 50

tactics 59–60
tattoos **9** (8), **17** (16)
thalassocracy 15–16, **45** (44)
Theokaris 12
Thera 19, 27, 39, 41, 51, 60
Theseus 54
Thessaly 12, 35, 37, 46
Thucydides 15, 16
tools 4, 6, 28, 36, 50
Troy 15, 36, 40, 47, 60
Tsountas 12

vases **29**, 34, 39, **42**, 43
votive objects **18**, 36, 58
Vounous 26

warfare 10, 13, 46, 51, 54–55, 59–60
warriors 10, **21** (20), **30**, 31, 51, 52, **53** (52), **58**, 59
weaponry 4, 6, 7, 12, 13, 14, 23–24, 58, 59; axes **8**, **9** (8), **27**, 35–36, 37, 50; bows and arrows **9** (8), 37–38, 48; daggers 6, **9** (8), **10**, **13**, 15, 18, 23, 28–32, 34–35, **36**, 47, 49; hammerheads **28**, 36; javelins 24, 26–8; knives **14**; maces 36; slings 35; spears **9** (8), **10**, **14**, 15, **17** (16), 24, 26–8, **33** (32), 47; swords **21** (20), **22**, 23, **24**, 27, 28–32, 46, 52, **53** (52), 54–55
women 13, **17** (16), **25** (24), **33** (32), 54, 58

Zakros 28, 30, 39, 42, **44**